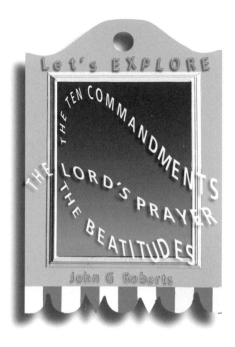

Let's EXPLORE

THE THE TEN COMMANDMENTS

THE LORD'S PRAYER

THE BEATITUDES

John G Roberts

DayOne

© Day One Publications 1999
First printed 1999

Scripture quotations are from The New King James Version.
© 1982 Thomas Nelson Inc.

British Library Cataloguing in Publication Data available
ISBN 0 902548 87 5

Published by Day One Publications
3 Epsom Business Park, Kiln Lane, Epsom, Surrey KT17 1JF.
☎ 01372 728 300 **FAX** 01372 722 400
e-mail address: ldos.dayone@ukonline.co.uk

Designed by Steve Devane.
Printed by Clifford Frost Limited, Wimbledon London SW19

Dedication
This book is dedicated to my
grandson Jacob, born during
the writing of this book.
My prayer is that God's Word may
become precious to him.

Inside *Let's Explore...*

Danny and **Karen** are thirteen year old twins; **Rachel** is a school friend of Karen's and she joins them for bible discussion on Sunday afternoons. With the help of the twins' parents, the three young people show how the Bible speaks to us today.

This book is divided into three parts; The Ten Commandments, The Lord's Prayer, and The Beatitudes.

Page 7

Part 1
Let's Explore
The Ten Commandments
In book one, they begin by discussing each of the Ten Commandments.

Page 69

Part 2
Let's Explore The Lord's Prayer
In book two, Danny and Karen look at every verse in the Lord's Prayer, and discover its relevance for today.

Page 125

Part 3
Let's Explore The Beatitudes
In book three, while on a canal boat holiday, the family get together to talk about the teaching of Jesus found in the Beatitudes.

Contents

Karen and Danny bring home ten questions

Karen bounded through the front door ahead of Danny and threw her rucksack on the floor. "I don't agree with him at all!" "Wait a minute Karen," her brother responded, "he may have a point. We should at least think about what he said."

"He was disagreeing with all that we have been taught at home and at church," Karen quickly replied before Danny could defend his teacher further."

"Hang on," said Danny when Karen briefly paused for breath. "We must consider his point of view fairly and honestly."

"But he wasn't being fair or honest," replied Karen as her mother entered the room, closely followed by the family pet - a collie named Lassie.

Mrs. Watson had just returned from her last call of the afternoon. For a number of years she had worked in Southwest London as a District Nurse.

"Hey, you two, what's the problem?" she enquired.

They both began to answer the question together, raising their voices in their excitement.

"Quiet! I can't understand both of you at the same time. Danny, you tell me the reason for this argument."

Danny and Karen were twins, with Danny being the elder by no more than five minutes. They were thirteen years of age, but Danny was more thoughtful and less impulsive than his lively sister. He was a tall boy and well built with curly hair. His sister was slim with long hair tumbling over her shoulders.

Danny began to explain that Mr. Dobson, their R.E. teacher, had brought up the subject of the Ten Commandments, but questioned whether they were really helpful for people today.

"Danny and Karen were twins, with Danny being the elder by no more than five minutes. They were thirteen years of age…"

Karen and Danny normally respected Mr. Dobson, although sometimes his views surprised them. Danny continued to give a detailed explanation of the events with Karen adding her own comments quite forcibly. Evidently Mr. Dobson had hinted that the Ten Commandments only applied to the Jews and the Old Testament, and were not fitting for today. This had raised many questions in Karen and Danny's minds, which resulted in the discussion now being related to their mother.

Eventually, after listening to her children's description of the lesson, Mrs. Watson suggested that they let the matter rest until their father returned from the City. Then, after tea they could talk through their questions with him.

Mr. Watson arrived home at six o'clock. He worked in London for an Insurance Company and his responsibilities often kept him late at the office. This particular evening, though, the tasks were completed in good time and he was home at a reasonable hour.

As his car reversed into the drive, Lassie immediately expressed her pleasure by standing at the door with her tail wagging at great speed. As soon as the front door opened, the dog leapt into Mr. Watson's arms in excitement. She was very much part of the family and lay beside Mr. Watson's chair while they had tea together.

Mr. Watson was a quiet, but friendly man, who knew his Bible well. He listened carefully to both Karen and Danny and after a short pause to consider the matters raised, he made the following suggestion.

"The Ten Commandments cover various subjects which are very important and should not be dismissed without careful thought. They refer to many different matters which concern people living today just as much as in Old Testament times."

"I told you so!" interrupted Karen as she looked at Danny with satisfaction realising that her father had agreed with her view.

"Now Karen, it's rude to butt in like that when your father is talking," said Mrs. Watson firmly and with a look that immediately conveyed to Karen her mother's displeasure. "Let your father finish, and then you can comment."

"As I was saying, the Ten Commandments cannot be passed by without understanding what the Bible has to say about them. If the Bible shows they are only meant for the age in which they were written, then we can dismiss them. But if we find out that God intended them to be meaningful today, then it would be wrong to ignore them."

> **"If the Bible shows they are only meant for the age in which they were written, then we can dismiss them. But if we find out that God intended them to be meaningful today, then it would be wrong to ignore them."**

Karen, always full of enthusiasm, interrupted again, this time with care, not wishing to receive another rebuke from her mother.

"Could I suggest," she said with quiet confidence, "that we discuss the Ten Commandments; it would help us with our R.E. lesson."

"Yes!" exclaimed Danny, surprised that he was actually agreeing with his sister. "That would help us both and it would be interesting to see what answers we come to."

Although Karen and Danny were twins, they each had their own particular hobbies and interests. Karen especially enjoyed skating and reading while Danny liked most sports, particularly cricket, and stamp collecting. However, in one thing they were completely agreed and that was to clear in their minds the important questions that Mr. Dobson's controversial remarks had raised.

"Let me take it further," Mr. Watson commented. "What about looking at one Commandment each Sunday afternoon for the next eleven weeks?"

"That has me puzzled," said Danny pulling his face.

"What's the problem?" asked his father, guessing his son's next question.

"I thought there were Ten Commandments, so why do we need eleven Sunday afternoons?"

Mr. Watson suggested that it would be helpful on the first Sunday to look at the Commandments together to see the importance of them as a group. This would give a good foundation for more detailed discussion.

Karen still sat with a concerned look on her face.

"Are you pleased with our suggestion?" asked her mother.

"Oh yes!" replied Karen. "It's just that my best friend in class is also puzzled. Most of the others don't care, or probably never even listened to what Mr. Dobson said, but Rachel did ask what we thought and, as you know, we were confused by Mr. Dobson's views."

"Ask Rachel if she would like to come for the afternoon. She can stay for tea and come to the evening service with us," suggested her mother.

"Oh, I'm not sure about that," interrupted Karen quickly. "She doesn't even go to Sunday school. It's just that she seemed so interested and it was difficult to explain."

"Ask her to come for the discussion and stay for tea, then she can leave afterwards," said Mr. Watson.

"That would be great," responded Karen.

Mr. Watson reminded his children that there was such a thing as homework and they should get on with it immediately. Karen and Danny went to their rooms but could not forget Mr. Dobson's talk, which had started their evening discussion.

Karen, Danny and Rachel find some answers

The sky was clear with just a few white, puffy clouds in the distance as the Watsons returned from church. The sun was hot so they were thankful for the gentle breeze which made the walk quite enjoyable.

Mr. and Mrs. Watson had bought their semi-detached house when they came to live in a suburb of Surrey. Originally they had lived in North Yorkshire, but Mr. Watson's work had brought them south. The house was situated in a quiet street with an avenue of trees along the roadside and during the summer their green leaves left attractive dappled shadows along the path.

"I hope dinner won't take long, mum," remarked Danny as they opened the front door.

"Make a cup of coffee please and that will help me work more quickly," replied his mother. "Before you sit down Karen, the table can be laid."

It wasn't long before the dinner was ready and even less time before it was eaten.

"I feel better now," said Danny as he relaxed in the chair with great satisfaction.

"Hey, dishes don't wash themselves," said Mr. Watson with a smile.

"You wash, I'll dry," suggested Danny to Karen as they made their way to the kitchen.

Soon the task was completed and it wasn't long before the doorbell rang. Karen rushed to the porch and greeted Rachel bringing her into the lounge.

It was becoming very hot and humid, so Danny opened some windows to let in as much air as possible. He then leapt into one of the

"Karen rushed to the porch and greeted Rachel bringing her into the lounge…"

armchairs hoping to claim it for the afternoon. It was in his possession less than two minutes before Mr. Watson entered the room. It only needed a look in Danny's direction before he took the hint and settled on the beanbag. Lassie, who always preferred someone on her level, soon snuggled up to Danny who began to stroke her under the ear. Lassie loved that. Karen and Rachel stretched out on the settee in the most comfortable positions possible.

"OK!" said Mr. Watson. "Let's begin our discussion and find out if Mr. Dobson is right or wrong in his suggestion that the Ten Commandments are not needed today. Now I will probably do most of the talking, but I don't want to dominate the conversation too much. We all must share in the discussion and express whatever thoughts or doubts we may have. The Ten Commandments were given to Moses on Mount Sinai, but had God shown any of their standards earlier?"

"Yes," Danny answered in a hesitating manner. "Wasn't He angry with Cain for killing Abel?"

"That's correct," replied his father, encouraged by the fact that so early in the discussion, one mind at least was beginning to work.

Then like a shot from a gun, Karen joined in eagerly.

"What about Jacob who wanted Esau's birthright?"

"Do you realise Karen," said Mr. Watson with a chuckle, "you have two examples in your one suggestion?"

"Have I?" replied Karen with surprise and pride mingled into one.

"Jacob coveted - and then stole Esau's birthright," emphasised Mr. Watson.

"Just a minute!" interrupted Mrs. Watson. "We must not forget the Sabbath Day. Before the Ten Commandments were given, God told Israel to collect manna for five days and on the sixth day to collect a double portion so that none would be collected on the seventh day, as it was their Sabbath."

"That's a very good example," said Mr. Watson, secretly disappointed that his wife had thought of it before he had.

There was a moment of quiet, but no further examples came. Mr. Watson then explained more fully how the Ten Commandments contained laws, which had been in existence from Creation. God had made them permanent by speaking them, writing them on stone tablets and instructing Moses to put them in the Ark of the Covenant.[1]

Before Mr. Watson could say more, Rachel, who was still a little shy of joining in, suddenly asked a question, hoping it was not out of place.

"I have heard people say that God gave the Ten Commandments to make life hard for us and order us about. My question may not be put very well, but do you see what I mean?"

Then because she felt unable to express herself clearly, Rachel wished she hadn't spoken.

Before she became too downcast, Mr. Watson assured her that he understood, and what she said deserved an explanation.

"Rachel has raised something important," he said. "When I was younger, I served in the British Army. Our Sergeant Major was a fine man, and we respected him very much. This, however, did not stop him from giving orders, which had to be obeyed. If we didn't do as he told us, we would get into a real mess as soon as a difficult problem occurred."

He paused to try and make it more personal. Then another thought came to him.

"Take our family as an example. Sometimes I have to correct Karen and Danny."

"Don't we know it," whispered Danny with a grin.

"I shall ignore that comment," he added with a wink in Danny's direction. "When I tell off these two rascals, it isn't because I want to spoil their fun. It is because I love them and want them to learn how to be really happy. Love and discipline go hand in hand in a happy home. God gives His Commandments, not to make life difficult, or unpleasant, but to make it better; He gave them because He loves us. Everything God gives is for our good, even the Commandments."

"I understand that now," said Rachel with a more relaxed face.

"Can I ask a question that puzzles me, at least I think it does?" said Karen.

"Go on, Karen," said her father.

"Are all the Commandments important today? I mean can some be forgotten? I know we mustn't kill or steal..."

"Or covet my computer games," interrupted Danny.

"Shut up!" Karen shouted trying to ignore her brother's taunt. "Is it possible to keep eight or nine, but forget the others?"

"That is a good point to raise," said Mr. Watson, now encouraged that all were joining in and asking questions. "Your mother has a string of pearls. If I cut the string what would happen?"

"They would all slip off the thread," answered Rachel.

"That's correct," agreed Mr. Watson. "You could lose them all. It is the same with the Commandments. Disobey one and in the end we could disobey them all."[2]

"I can't see that," said Danny with a puzzled expression.

Mr. Watson then gave an example, explaining that wanting something that belongs to someone else is a form of coveting. If Karen really wanted a book belonging to Danny, she may try to steal it and then tell lies to cover up what she had done, perhaps by blaming someone else. That would be three Commandments that had been broken."

"I never thought of it like that before," said Karen.

"Neither did I," joined in Danny and Rachel together.

The discussion continued until Mrs. Watson had to suggest coming to a close so tea could be prepared.

"I never thought I could enjoy discussing a subject such as the Ten Commandments," said Danny with surprise.

"You learn by sharing views," replied his father, "We all have much to learn."

"Even you?" questioned Karen.

"Even me," said Mr. Watson with a smile.

In the first Commandment, God instructs us to have no other gods before Him

The week at school seemed to go quickly. Karen enjoyed her studies, particularly science. Her favourite was biology, probably because she wanted to be a nurse when she left school. Danny, however, wasn't all that keen, especially when it involved homework. He always said that he shouldn't have to work longer hours than the teachers especially when he wasn't paid for it. From a very young age he wanted to be in the police force and this desire stayed with him. His uncle held a high position within the Yorkshire police, and he looked forward to following in his footsteps.

Sunday eventually arrived and it was another hot day, without a cloud in sight. A breeze would have been most welcome, but the trees stood still and tall like soldiers on parade.

"Can we sit outside this afternoon?" asked Karen.

"I can't see why not," replied her mother, "as long as the garden chairs are put in the shade."

Mr. Watson always wore a suit and tie to work and to the church service. As soon as he returned home from church, however, not only did the jacket come off, but also the tie!

The doorbell rang and Rachel arrived a little earlier than expected.

"You're enthusiastic!" said Mrs. Watson as she greeted Rachel.

"I hope I'm not too early," she said anxiously.

"Not at all, you're very welcome."

"Kathy," said Mr. Watson to his wife, "could you bring glasses of cool orange? We'll need to keep our throats moist with all the talking we'll be doing."

Soon drinks were prepared, complete with ice-cubes, and Mrs.

Watson brought them into the garden on a large tray. She was closely followed by Lassie who was finding the heat uncomfortable because of her thick coat. She found a place to lay out of the direct sun and was soon asleep.

When everyone else had settled, Mr. Watson read the first Commandment from his Bible, which said that we must have no other gods before the true God.

"The children of Israel knew God's blessing upon them when they put Him first. When they allowed other gods to take His place, then God had to warn them and sometimes punish them"

He began by reminding them that during the years in Egypt, many foreign gods who were worshipped by the Egyptians had surrounded the Israelites. Now God was reminding them that He was the only true God and that He must take first place above everything else.

"I suppose He is saying the same thing to us today," suggested Danny.

"That's right. Nothing must come before Him. You see, the children of Israel knew God's blessing upon them when they put Him first. When they allowed other gods to take His place, then God had to warn them and sometimes punish them."

Mrs. Watson appreciated listening to the conversation, and very rarely interrupted. When she did make a statement it usually caused the others to think very carefully.

"I was thinking about this Commandment yesterday, and the decision I came to was that, if we love something else more than God, we cannot be His followers. He must come first."

After a pause to think about what her mother had said, Karen asked with concern in her voice, "is it wrong to have hobbies?"

"What do you think Rachel?" asked Mr. Watson, not wanting to

"Soon drinks were prepared, complete with ice-cubes, and Mrs. Watson brought them into the garden on a large tray. When everyone else had settled, Mr. Watson read from his Bible the first Commandment, which said that we must have no other gods before the true God…"

leave their guest out of the discussion.

"It can't be wrong, can it? But I suppose hobbies can use up a great deal of time if you are not careful."

"No one could have answered the question better," replied Mr. Watson enthusiastically.

Rachel's face flushed with pride. She was delighted with Mr.

Watson's praise, and listened carefully as he went on to say, "Hobbies are not wrong in themselves, but we need to make sure that we do not spend too much time on them and let them become more important than anything else in our lives."

"When I was much younger," said Rachel, "my cousin went with her school to Austria, and she brought me back a doll in National costume. Since then, I drop hints to friends who go abroad that the souvenir I would most like is a foreign doll. They look really nice displayed in my bedroom."

"That's fine," continued Mr. Watson. "I know Danny is keen on stamp collecting and Karen on ice skating. All these things are good as long as you don't put them first and in effect, worship them."

"You see, people are born with the need to worship. Everyone will worship something or even someone," said Mr. Watson, slightly changing the discussion from things to people. "What about the film or pop stars?"

"Tennis, football and cricket," continued Danny in case his father was short of examples.

The conversation continued on this theme for quite some time and all present acknowledged that young and old alike had to be careful and ensure that God must take first place above everything else if we are to follow Him closely.

Time passed very quickly and although Mr. Watson was pleased with the discussion, there was one important point that he wanted to emphasise.

"We have talked about the importance of having no other gods, because there is no other god. We cannot worship the Lord and serve other gods. A wife cannot have two husbands at once, nor can we have two gods."

"I'm not sure I could manage one husband if he needs looking after like Danny," said Karen with a broad grin.

"Now then, we'll have none of that," Mr. Watson replied with an equally broad grin. "I see your mother is ready to prepare something to eat."

"Whether she is or not, I'm getting ready for it," interrupted Danny. "Go on, Dad, it's been good and caused me to think more than ever before about this."

"Let me ask a question. We have thought about the first Commandment in Exodus Chapter 20, but where do we read of a more important first Commandment?"

"It must be somewhere in the New Testament," answered Rachel hopefully.

"Correct!" said Mr. Watson, reassuring Rachel that she had not made a mistake. "But where?"

The three youngsters looked at each other, but no suggestion came.

"In Matthew[3], Mark[4] and Luke[5] we are told to love God with all our heart, soul, mind and strength. But how do we do this?"

"By reading the Bible," said Karen.

"By saying our prayers," joined in Danny.

"I suppose by going to church," said Rachel, "Although I don't often go. My father says he can worship God on the golf course on Sunday mornings."

"There is a big difficulty here, Rachel, and that is, what happens when trouble comes – such as losing someone close to us? Do we go to the golf course to be comforted? No! We go to church, but we can't have God as a medicine bottle just in case problems come. We must put Him first in sunshine and rain."

"I never realised that, but I think I do now," Rachel answered.

"In putting God first we must read our Bible and pray every day, and regularly go to church to worship Him," said Mr. Watson.

"Could I go with you tonight?" asked Rachel, very interested by the afternoon discussion.

"Sure" Karen exclaimed.

"We'll ring your parents now and see if you can stay to tea. Then I can take you home after the service," replied Mrs. Watson. "Come on Karen, set the table quickly or else we shall be late."

In the second Commandment, God instructs us that we should not make any carved image

"What a change in the weather," Mrs. Watson said to her husband as they got ready for church the following Sunday morning. The whole country had enjoyed high temperatures for over a week reaching 27°C. However, during the last two days clouds had covered the sun so although it was still hot it had become very humid and uncomfortable.

"I wouldn't be surprised if we have a storm," he replied.

He had hardly uttered the words before large drops of rain began to run down the windows. Very soon it began to pour heavily.

"It won't help my hair to grow, but it will do the lawns good," he said jokingly. "I'll get the car out or we will be soaked before we get to church."

By the time they returned home, the rain had eased and the wind began to gently move the branches of the trees lining the roadside. The family soon sat down for lunch with windows and doors wide open to enjoy what breeze was available.

"Come on!" said Danny, "Let's get these dishes washed so we can continue our discussions."

"I can't believe what I'm hearing," said Karen with obvious shock. "He's never suggested doing this before."

"I didn't suggest I was doing them, but I will supervise."

"The only place you will supervise is in the sink," said Mr. Watson with a sly wink at his wife.

"I like that," laughed Karen.

"I hope you like my second suggestion that you supervise the drying. Here's the tea towel."

"It wasn't long before both tasks were completed and in the meantime Rachel had arrived.

"I really enjoyed last Sunday afternoon," she told Mr. Watson. Our discussions have made me think."

"I'm so pleased Rachel. They are teaching me a great deal also."

The chairs in the lounge were soon occupied and Mr. Watson turned everyone's attention to the second Commandment.

"In many ways there are clear likenesses between this and the first Commandment, but it is different. In the first Commandment we are not to worship false gods and in this second Commandment we are not to worship the true God in a false way."

After this opening statement, he then went on to show the dangers of using images to worship God. He explained "that God is invisible and can only be known in a spiritual way. If we know God as someone real and living, we do not need images in our prayers. We see God by faith and not by things. God is far greater than we can imagine, so how can we show His glory in images?"

He then turned in his Bible to John chapter four and verse 24, and read to them: "God is a Spirit and they that worship Him must worship Him in spirit and in truth." To make a true image of God is impossible because He is a Spirit and invisible. To bow to an image of God when He is present everywhere is foolish."

"Rachel, you are good at art so I hear. Paint a picture of my brother in South Africa," requested Mr. Watson.

"I can't. I've never seen him," she replied.

"That's the answer I expected. We cannot make an image or likeness of someone we have never seen. My brother would be very upset if he received a picture that wasn't like him. So we can't describe God—who is life—by that which is without life. It seems daft to me to compare the Maker of all by something which is made."

"I haven't heard you use the word 'daft' for many years," said Mrs. Watson with a smile.

"Northern upbringing you know," he replied.

"I know what it means Dad," said Danny reassuringly. "We use it at school often."

"Anyway, do you understand what I am saying?"

They all nodded their heads in agreement which gave Mr. Watson a great deal of encouragement.

There were a few moments of silence before Mrs. Watson made one of her rare but carefully thought out contributions.

"We have considered that other gods or images are made by our hands, but God made all things out of nothing. Yet the gods we make can't help us, can't speak, can't hear, can't think, can't act, can't see and above all else, can't love. Our God, who is living, can do all these things and more."

"I never thought of it like that," acknowledged Rachel.

"I have just been reading in my quiet time the Book of Kings," said Karen. "I can't pronounce all the names, but it tells how the evil kings in Israel and Judah made idols and worshipped them, and then the good kings destroyed them."

"That's right," confirmed Mr. Watson. "It just shows how the Bible speaks against image worship."

"There is one thing I'm not sure about," said Karen, curling a few strands of hair around one of her fingers.

"What's that?" asked her father.

"How can we think of God without images? What I really mean is, can we have images of Christ because He did become man?"

"That's true," replied her father. "But remember, He is also God. To picture Him as a man when we cannot picture Him as God will make Him only half Christ."

"It's difficult, but I think I understand," said Karen.

"I think it will help if I answer your first question," Mr. Watson continued. "We can think of God by looking at His characteristics. God is holy, He is good, He is faithful, and He is love. I could go on with many more. You don't need images when you think of God in this way."

"How should we worship?" asked Danny.

"That's a good question to finish with," stated his father realising they must soon come to a close.

Danny relaxed back in his chair after being complimented in that way. He very soon sat straight when his father replied.

"You have asked the question, now see if you can answer it."

After a slight pause he found the answer.

"Thanking God in prayer, then reading the Bible and listening to a teacher or a preacher."

> "...the gods we make can't help us, can't speak, can't hear, can't think, can't act, can't see and above all else, can't love. Our God, who is living, can do all these things and more..."

"Any other ideas?" asked Mr. Watson looking at the others.

"Singing praises," suggested Rachel, "because I like doing that very much."

"Can I have the last word?" asked Mrs. Watson.

"You usually do dear," said her husband with a smile.

"Don't you think we have been worshipping God as a family, and I include you Rachel, during these past few Sunday afternoons?"

"Yes," said Danny, "and with no images to help us."

"Karen, it's time to boil the kettle or we'll be rushing for church," said her mother.

"How do you do that?" asked Karen with a sly grin.

"What do you mean?"

"It's the water that boils, not the kettle."

"Go on with you," laughed her father ready to rise from his chair and chase her into the kitchen.

In the third Commandment, God instructs us that we should not take His Name in vain

T he following Sunday came round quickly. The three children were studying for their exams, which would soon be upon them, so they valued one day when they could forget revision. On the positive side they looked forward to their afternoon discussions. They appreciated their daily quiet time, but never realised how enjoyable it could be to share thoughts about a subject such as the Ten Commandments.

"Before you open your Bibles, tell me the third Commandment," asked Mr. Watson as he settled comfortably in his chair.

Without hesitation, Danny recited it with confidence, afterwards admitting that he read it while dinner was being prepared.

Mr. Watson opened the subject by saying that when we speak about God, we must be sincere and respectful. His Name should always be respected, and kept holy in thought, word and deed. This will prevent us from misusing His name by having wrong thoughts or swearing. When we use His Name it must be to His glory or to the benefit of those we are speaking to. We must always have honourable thoughts of Him. "By the way, do you know the most dangerous weapon on this earth?" asked Mr. Watson.

The question surprised the youngsters, as it seemed to be leading to a different topic. Nevertheless, they responded with suggestions from guns to bombs.

"You are all wrong," he replied after listening to their answers. "The most dangerous weapon is our tongue."

"I never thought of that," said Rachel after careful consideration.

"I'm afraid it's true," continued Mr. Watson. "Just notice how

God's name is used in a bad way. At one time we never heard it this way except by a few, but today it is heard on the media by millions. Now it is spoken in the streets, at work, school and even in the home. Expressions such as 'My God' or 'For Christ's sake do this or that' are regularly used."

"Can I share an experience I had a few weeks ago?" interrupted Mrs. Watson.

Before anyone had time to reply to her question she began to tell her story.

"A few weeks ago, I was visiting a certain home and as we were boiling the water, the fuse went. Immediately the husband used God's Name in a wrong way. Although I didn't say anything, he saw that I was upset. It gave me the chance to explain that as I was a Christian, it hurt me to hear the One I loved being spoken of in that way. He apologised and confessed that he hadn't thought about it like that before and he would be more careful in future."

"Danny, do you remember that youth meeting when the speaker told us details of his conversion?" asked Karen.

"Yes I do," replied Danny. "Rachel hasn't heard it, and mum and dad were too old to be there. Only joking!" Danny quickly hid his face behind a cushion.

"Go on," said Mr. Watson with a smile. "Let's hear it without further cheeky comments."

"There was a pastor of a small church in Kent who owned a garage which had a showroom of new and second-hand cars. A customer bought a new car and evidently had trouble with it. He returned it to the garage and in the pastor's office used terrible language, including God's Name as a form of swearing. The pastor quietly told him that he could do something for the car but only God could put his tongue right. During further visits to the garage, they both had long chats and it resulted in the gentleman becoming a Christian."

"That's a good story," responded Mr. Watson. "It just shows that we must make a witness to those who misuse God's Name."

"Surely it can't be easy to do that," suggested Karen hesitatingly. "I know people who would just laugh at me and do it even more."

"That's true," answered Mr. Watson, "but when we love Jesus we cannot remain silent. We should be a witness to those who use His Name in a wrong way. You see, Rachel, we have to look at this negatively and positively. The negative says we must not use God's Name in a wrong way. The positive tells us to honour His Name and hold it up high in our thoughts."

Mrs. Watson kept glancing at her daughter who seemed deep in thought.

"A penny for your thoughts, Karen."

"Oh, they are worth much more than that. I was just wondering if we, who love God, can be careless in using His Name."

"Yes, I'm sure we can," said her mother. "I remember a few years ago when I went to court as a witness to a road accident. When I had to promise to tell the truth, I wanted to be sure I was totally honest. I didn't want to say something was true when I didn't know if it was or not. Sometimes we exaggerate a story to impress our hearers, which is really another form of lying. Exaggeration is a great sin, especially when we have called upon God to witness our statement. We need to be careful how we testify. In Zechariah chapter 8 and verse 17 we are told that God hates lying. Remember the more a man tells untruths, the less others will believe him."

"I never thought of it that way," commented Danny. "I suppose we can make false oaths anywhere and not just in court."

"We can look at it another way," said Mr. Watson as Danny continued to think about his statement. "People take God's Name in vain when they profess to be Christians and are not. In Luke chapter 6 and verse 46 Jesus asked the people why they called him Lord and refused to do what he said."

"I suppose that's hypocrisy," suggested Danny.

"That's a big word, Danny, but you are right," continued his father. "It is speaking to God with our lips when our hearts are far from

Him. To take it to the extreme, it is completely wrong for an ungodly person to speak of God at all."

"But do people mean any harm by using God's Name in a wrong way?" asked Rachel. "They say others do it and it makes them feel better."

"Well, Rachel," replied Mr. Watson, "let's look at the Royal Family for example, or other people in the country who hold high positions.

"God is greatly hurt by this sin and the guilty will be punished in God's time. Let us ensure we never use God's Name carelessly"

When we speak to them or about them we give them their full title or honour. They would be hurt and even angry if their names were abused. Shouldn't we then speak with greater respect of the King of Heaven who is our Creator? People so often use God's Name in careless conversation. They have God in their mouth, but not in their heart."

The afternoon had once again gone quickly by and Mr. Watson had to conclude the discussion.

"Two facts are clear from our time this afternoon. The first is that it is almost impossible to walk the city streets or be with an ordinary group of people without hearing God's sacred Name being ill-treated. It is also abused in books, on radio and television, in the theatre and cinema, and the newspapers are not completely innocent. The second fact is that God is greatly hurt by this sin and the guilty will be punished in God's time. Let us ensure we never use God's Name carelessly. If we love Him, we will also love His Name."

"Now, jump to it you three," instructed Mrs. Watson. "Lassie would welcome a walk before we get ready for church."

As soon as the word 'walk' was mentioned, the dog jumped to her feet and barked excitedly as she made her way with the youngsters to the door.

In the fourth Commandment, God instructs us to remember the Sabbath Day to keep it holy

"**D**o you know what we talked about in R.E. last Wednesday?" asked Danny, as he and his father walked into the lounge on the following Sunday afternoon.

"No, but I can guess. Was it one of the Commandments we have already discussed?"

"Wrong, I'm afraid," replied Danny. "Mr. Dobson had us discussing the subject for this afternoon, the Sunday question. Don't say anything to Karen or Rachel, but I guess they will mention it sometime during the afternoon."

"Well, we won't have long to wait and see if you are right, because here they come."

The two girls entered the room chatting away as if nobody else was present. Karen and Rachel had always been friends, but these Sunday afternoons had made their friendship even stronger.

"If you are all comfortable we can turn to the fourth Commandment. Now this is a very important one, not just because it is the longest, but because it links the first three, which we have already talked about, with the following six. The first three tell us about our relationship with God, and the remaining six tell us about our relationship with other people. The fourth Commandment does both, by showing us how we should love God and how we should behave with our neighbour. The place of the Sabbath in our lives, therefore, is very important."

"Mr. Dobson said we shouldn't use that word, because it is Jewish and another word for Saturday," interrupted Karen.

Danny and his Father's eyes met. With a slight nod of the head, Mr.

Watson acknowledged that his son had guessed correctly. He then went on to explain the meaning of the word.

"The term 'Sabbath' does not mean Saturday, but rest, pause and stop work. It is, therefore, correct to call Sunday the Sabbath, as it is the day when Christians rest from their daily work and meet to worship God. God gave a day of rest at creation [6] for all people and not just for the Jews. It does not say in the Commandment or anywhere else 'the seventh day of the week', but on the 'seventh day'. With the Jews, it is the seventh day of the week, but with Christians it is the first day."

"Why did it then become the first day of the week?" asked Karen with keen interest.

"That's an important question and takes us to the very heart of the subject," replied her father. "The day changed following the resurrection of our Lord. Ever since that great event, the apostles met together on the first day [7], and the Christian Church has continued in the same way. You see, Karen, God's power was shown when He made us, but He demonstrated greater power when He saved us. It cost more to save us than create us. The creation of the world was a miracle, but the fact that Jesus died and rose again to forgive our sin was an even greater miracle. Does that brief explanation help you?"

"Yes, I can understand it better now."

"Can I ask a question?"

"Go on Rachel, I can see Mr. Dobson has got your mind ticking over on this subject.

"If God made every day, surely all days have the same importance; we can worship God any day and at any time. Why is Sunday to be different?"

"Can I try to answer this, Rachel, while my husband gets us all a cool drink of orange?" interrupted Mrs. Watson. "Of course we can worship God on any day, but because of work and other commitments, it is not practical for the family to spend another day apart from Sunday in worship. God made all days, but He made one different from all the others. When Adam was created, he was perfect. If a perfect man needed a day of rest and worship, how much more do we who are not perfect need this special day."

"But some people have to work on Sundays," stated Danny.

"That's true," confirmed his father. "The Bible allows for tasks that are necessary. Let's take Karen as an example. Very soon she hopes to begin training as a nurse. Caring for the sick is called an act of mercy. We need to have doctors, nurses and medical staff available on Sundays looking after the sick and elderly. Danny can be used as another example. To uphold law and order, it is necessary for the police to work on Sunday, as it is for firemen. There are people who need to work on Sunday for everyone's benefit, but that should only be for essential work. We should ensure that as many people as possible have Sunday as a day for worship, rest and to be with their families, which is so important."

As they were talking together a deafening noise was heard outside. Danny immediately rushed to the window and then shouted that there had been an accident. Mrs. Watson asked them to pass her first aid bag and quickly rushed to the scene. A car and motorbike had collided and it was clear to her that an ambulance was needed. She asked her husband to ring for one and told Danny to get her some rugs and blankets.

In a very short time the young motorcyclist was made comfortable until the ambulance arrived. Mrs. Watson then noticed the driver of the car was wandering around in a dazed condition. She realised that he was in a state of shock and asked her husband to take him inside and make him a hot cup of tea.

Within minutes, the ambulance came to the scene and the rider was carefully laid on a stretcher, badly cut and bruised but apparently with no broken bones. In the house the police were talking to the driver who was feeling a little more relaxed though still shaken. After he had given a statement the police thanked Mr. and Mrs. Watson for their swift action.

"You did stay calm, Mum," said Karen after the unexpected visitors had left.

"This was a minor crisis compared to many others, but we must do what we can to help in any situation. We know Jesus would have acted with compassion whether or not it was the Sabbath"

It took some time to pick up the subject again, but Karen was keen for her father to reply to her teacher's arguments.

"Mr. Dobson said we have laws to protect Sunday, but they are in a mess."

> "If God gave us six days to fill with busy activity, should we rob Him of part of His day? The whole day should be given to Him."

"It is true that we have laws to guard our Sunday," replied her father. "They are clear but are not always applied consistently. People might not agree with them but they are needed. God's Laws are even more important. Most of the evil things in our country come from the fact that we fail to keep God's Commandments. The greatness of this country has not been built on military power, or business success, but on moral and Christian standards which include a respect for God's Day. Parliament did not give Sunday to the Nation, but Parliament has a responsibility to protect it."

"I hope we don't spoil Sunday," said Danny.

"So do I," agreed his mother.

"Now I want to ask a question," stated Mr. Watson. "What is different about this Commandment, apart from it being the longest as I mentioned earlier?"

"It begins with the word 'remember,'" suggested Rachel.

"That's correct, it's positive," said Mr. Watson. "The problem with people is that they easily forget."

"I know," said Karen, "I have a bad memory."

"In some things we all have," added her mother.

"Yes, that's true," continued her father. "God knows this, and that is why on such an important matter, He tells us to remember His Day and not forget to keep it holy."

"What about doing homework on a Sunday?" asked Rachel. "My parents say it doesn't matter when you do it as long as it has been done well."

Mrs. Watson thanked Rachel for raising an important issue. She then explained that Karen and Danny had been encouraged to complete their homework so that no studying was necessary on God's Day. We have a body that needs rest from physical work, but we also have a mind that needs a break from study. We are physically made to cope with work and study for six days, but it is vital to rest and unwind on the day God has given for this purpose. As God has made us, He knows best what we are capable of achieving. There was no doubt that students will produce better results if they put away their books for one day each week.

"As we have been talking about school, I heard on Friday that I could be selected to play against a local college at cricket."

Everyone immediately began to congratulate Danny on this news, but soon realised that doubts were in his mind.

"The problem is that the match will be played on Sunday morning."

"I'm very sorry that young people are being faced with this problem," said his father. "They should not have to decide between going to church or representing their school."

Mr. Watson intended speaking to the Headmaster about the matter, but also wanted to know how Danny felt about it.

Danny began to tell them about a video that he had seen based on the life of Eric Liddell, the Scotsman who refused to run in the Olympic Games on a Sunday. The film had made a big impression on him. Although Danny loved his cricket, as a Christian he felt he must put God first.

Danny's parents were very pleased with the way he had responded to this dilemma.

They all continued in conversation for quite a while, covering virtually every aspect of the Sunday question until Rachel raised a matter which had not been mentioned before.

"Some people say that if you go to church in the morning, the rest of the day can be spent as you choose."

"When we read the fourth Commandment," replied Mr. Watson, "it tells us to remember the Day and keep it holy, and not just for a few hours. If God gave us six days to fill with busy activity, should we rob Him of part of His day? The whole day should be given to Him."

"I'm afraid we must finish now, but before we do, can I tell you all something I read recently?" asked Mrs. Watson. "If we live on this earth for 70 years, we will have had ten years of Sundays. When I read that I had to ask myself how I would have spent those ten years?"

"It makes you think, Mum, but don't worry you have a few years to go yet," smiled Karen.

In the fifth Commandment, God instructs us to honour our father and mother

Rachel's parents had been invited to friends for the day, but as she would be the only young person there, permission was given for her to have dinner and tea with Mr. and Mrs. Watson instead.

"I'm so pleased you could come to dinner," said Karen tucking into her lemon meringue pie."

"So am I," replied Rachel. "It was kind of your mother to ask me."

"I hope you'll be as pleased when we have to wash the dishes," said Danny with a hearty laugh.

Soon the table was cleared, dishes washed and put away, and the chairs in the lounge occupied, although as on most occasions the girls sat on the floor. Lassie had been a little unsure of Rachel at first, but by now they had become firm friends. Whenever the girls sat on the floor Lassie would snuggle between them and in no time fall asleep.

"Now we come to the fifth Commandment," began Mr. Watson. "I feel this might be difficult, but I'm sure it will be interesting. Let me say at the very beginning, this Commandment goes much further than father and mother. It also includes ministers of the church, judges in court; in fact, all who have positions of authority. Having said that, we will just think of children and their relationship with their parents."

"I hope it doesn't sound rude," Karen interrupted, "but shouldn't we also look at parents and their relationship with their children?"

"That's a good point, Karen," replied her father. "I'll make sure that is not forgotten before we close."

Mr. Watson made a point of always carrying a small note pad, and to make sure he didn't forget, he wrote the comment down and laid the pad on the coffee table in front of him.

"When we read the Bible," Mr. Watson continued, "it is interesting to see the respect that is shown to parents. Although Joseph was ranked so highly in Egypt, we are told that he showed great respect to his father.[8] King Solomon was another who honoured his mother.[9] We are told in Proverbs to listen to parents' instructions."[10]

"What about the New Testament?" jumped in Danny trying to impress the family with his knowledge. "Only this week I was reading part of Matthew's Gospel and Jesus reminded the Pharisees of this Commandment.[11]"

"I'm sure you will find most of the Commandments confirmed in the New Testament," said his mother. "The most important person to emphasise them was the Lord Jesus who did so not just in word, but also by example.[12]"

"That's right," said Mr. Watson. "I made a note here to remind me of the Epistle to the Colossians [13] which tells us that in obeying our parents we are pleasing God. I hope I'm not giving you too many verses, but in Timothy [14] Paul tells us to provide, if possible, for our parents' old age."

"We had better start saving now," suggested Karen to Danny.

"I think we had better ask for an increase in pocket money," he replied.

Both their parents saw the funny side of the two comments, but Mr. Watson went on to explain the parents' responsibility when their children are young and the children's responsibility when parents become frail and elderly. To emphasise the children's duty, Mrs. Watson explained how young storks by an instinct of nature, bring food to the old ones when, because of age, they are unable to fly. The youngsters saw the point that was made.

"I think it is important before we go further to find out what the word 'honour' means," said Mr. Watson. "You are the nearest to the dictionary Rachel, so tell us what it says."

Rachel fumbled her way through the large book until she found the word.

"It means high respect, giving credit, and having a good name."

"That's fine," replied Mr. Watson. "We should love and respect our parents and do everything possible to preserve their good name. We must do nothing that would grieve them. Now I'll ask a question; how should we respect them?"

"I suppose by how we speak to them," answered Karen.

"By being obedient to all they tell us, and listening to their advice," joined in Danny.

"By caring for them," said Rachel not wanting to be left out.

"These are very good answers," said Mr. Watson trying to encourage the youngsters. "You see, to honour our parents is not a choice, it is a command of God. Parents bring their children up and care for them, which is a sign of love. In fact, some parents take more care of their children than they do of themselves. So they deserve honour because of their love and affection."

Rachel was quietly listening to all that was being said, but a puzzled look crossed her face. She wanted to ask a question, but did not want to look foolish if it was not sensible. However, Mrs. Watson, who was always quick to notice a change in someone's expression, encouraged Rachel to share her problem.

"I might not put this across clearly, but it's fairly easy in a Christian home like this to talk about obeying and respecting your parents because Karen and Danny would not be asked to do anything wrong. Although my parents hardly ever go to church, they have been good to me and I love and respect them. But what about children who are brought up in a home where there isn't love and where they are set a bad example? Do they obey their parents? I hope you know what I mean."

"That's a very good point, Rachel and I know what you are trying to say," replied Mr. Watson. "In fact, I think you have put it very clearly."

Mr. Watson began by looking at the sad situation in our country. For many tens of thousands of young people, family homes do not exist. Parents have separated or are divorced and children are unaware of even where a parent is living. Children are told to do things they know are wrong and a bad example is set. For children to obey in this situation is an insult to God's Command and will eventually have tragic results. It is important that these young people are encouraged to pray for their parents. When difficult times come they should also seek guidance from someone they can trust. This may be the minister of their church or a very close relative who would understand the problem. There are people who would be willing to help and give advice, and this would help them to know that they are not alone, but can have confidence in someone who has experience in these matters.

The discussion continued for some time until Mr. Watson remembered the note he had made earlier.

"I did promise to spend a few minutes considering how parents should act towards their children in order to gain their respect."

"Could I make a suggestion?" asked Mrs. Watson.

Again, the silent nodding of heads showed approval.

Mrs. Watson then continued to give eight steps for parents to gain their children's respect. The first was to bring them up to respect God. The second was to be kind but not spoil by giving love without discipline. The third was to provide for children when they are young and in need. The fourth to encourage them to come to them with any problem small or large. The fifth to treat all their children alike, with no favouritism. The sixth to encourage what is good and pleasing. The seventh to pray for them and the final to set a good example.

"How long did it take you to think of all those?" asked Karen.

"Although I have been listening to what you have been saying, I thought I would note these points as soon as your father said we would discuss a parent's role before we close."

"We must finish now," said Mr. Watson, "but I do feel we have been helped as a family from our afternoon together."

In the sixth Commandment, God instructs us not to kill

On the following Sunday after dinner, Danny entered the room with a large pad and pencil. "It's not the time to write a love letter," said his father jokingly.

"The pad is too small for that," replied Danny. "I want to write down important things because I'm sure to forget them knowing my memory. I can use them if they are discussed at school."

"Good idea," said his father. "I think you could be quite busy with the sixth Commandment."

As Rachel had just arrived everyone entered the lounge and soon settled into their usual places so the discussion could begin.

"As we look at this Commandment, we must remind ourselves of the words of Jesus. In Matthew's Gospel [15] He warns people against being angry without a reason for it. However, it can be correct to show anger and one example is when people use God's Name in a wrong way. Anger without a reason can eventually be the cause of murder. Who was the first person in the Bible to kill someone else?"

"Was it Cain?" asked Karen, hoping she was right.

"That's correct, but why did he do it?"

"Because he was jealous that God had accepted Abel's offering," answered Karen before anyone else could reply.

"Correct again," assured her father. "Now notice that on this occasion jealousy caused Abel's death. This command not only condemns the crime of murder, but also the reasons for it, such as jealousy, anger and hatred. You will find that very often one leads to the other. Let's look at Joseph for an example. His brothers were jealous when his father gave him a coat of many colours because he was a favourite son. Their jealousy soon led to anger, especially when he told them that, one day, they would bow down before him. Their anger then turned to hatred with suggestions that he should be killed. God, however, had other plans and Joseph's life was spared. There are many other examples when jealousy did eventually lead to someone dying, but I wonder if anyone can tell me the most important example?"

There was a moment of silence as the youngsters began to think of the possible answer. Eventually Rachel leapt to her feet with a confident reply.

"I've got it!"

"I wish I had," said Karen with a puzzled look on her face.

"It must have been Jesus," Rachel continued. "The Pharisees were jealous because bigger crowds went to hear Him. They were angry at what He said, and this led to hatred and His death."

"Well done," said Mr. Watson.

"Why didn't I think of that?" said Danny annoyed that he had not been quicker than Rachel.

"Of course," continued Mr. Watson, "we have always to remember that it was God's plan for Jesus to die. God knew there was no other way for us to be saved from our sin, but for Jesus to bear it on the cross for us."

Mr. Watson then went on to explain that anger, jealousy and hatred do not always break out suddenly, but they can develop gradually so that in the end it leads to violence and murder. What people see sometimes in films or read in books can eventually lead to someone's death. Today we spend money and time in controlling the actions of the body, but we need much more to protect the heart and mind. It is from these that evil comes. We must never forget that for someone to deliberately take a life is against God's law whether it is because of dislike, a robbery that turns to violence, or simply wanting that person out of the way."

"What about war?" asked Danny jumping in quickly. "There are many people being killed all over the world."

"That's an important question and not easy to answer. I read only recently that there are more than 30 wars taking place in the world at this very moment. No one with any sense wants war and we should never look for it. The results are grief and suffering. But we must remember that the shedding of blood in a just war cannot be classed as murder but is more like self-defence or defending others. If one country, for no other reason than wanting power, decides to take over another country, it must be prevented and sometimes the only way to do that is fighting in self-defence, and that is not murder. However, war must be a last resort when everything else has failed. I hope you can understand the difference as I realise it can be difficult."

Mr. Watson then continued to show that accidental killing, which means the person had no intention of doing so, is also not murder. In Deuteronomy [16] the story is told of a man who was cutting wood and the axe slipped killing his neighbour. God appointed cities of refuge where people who had killed accidentally could be safe.

"What then can be called murder?" asked Karen who had at first thought this would be an easy subject.

"Well, we have mentioned one earlier," replied her father. "It is murder when someone kills another intentionally through jealousy, hatred, greed or revenge. Another form of murder is suicide, which is self-murder."

"I never thought of that!" Karen exclaimed in surprise.

"This is probably one of the saddest crimes a person can commit," continued her father. "To make it more difficult, another form of murder is when a person is an accessory to the crime and I will explain that. This is when someone arranges for it to be done without doing it on his or her own. In the Second Book of Samuel [17] we have the story of David, who sent Uriah to the front line of battle so he could have his wife Bathsheba. You can also be an accessory to the crime by giving permission for someone's death. Come on, who did that?"

The three youngsters looked at each other but no response came. Mr. Watson then turned to his wife for the answer.

"Were you thinking of Pilate, who gave Jesus to be crucified, even though he knew Jesus was innocent?"

"That's right. He gave permission for the Jews to take Jesus."

The afternoon had again passed by very quickly but Mr. Watson had one more point to raise before they concluded.

"Apart from suicide, have you thought that there are other ways by which we can become guilty of our own death? This is when we put ourselves in danger carelessly or even intentionally."

"I'm not sure what you mean." said Rachel hoping the others were also confused.

"'On the following Sunday after dinner, Danny entered the room with a large pad and pencil. "I want to write down important things because I'm sure to forget them knowing my memory..."'

"Let me give you some examples. How about ignoring ways of staying healthy? Some people, if they are sick, use no remedy, they will not apply a cure. Smoking, drugs, excessive eating and heavy drinking shortens lives. My father used to say that some people live to eat and not eat to live."

"We have those at school," laughed Danny.

"Sometimes I think we have them here," said Mr. Watson, looking at Danny with a smile. "The point I am trying to make is that the Bible says the Holy Spirit lives within us, and we need to care for our bodies and not abuse them."

"I get it now," said Rachel with a sense of relief.

"What the Commandment is saying is that we have a responsibility to preserve our life and the lives of others. Life is very precious because God has given it to us." Mr. Watson concluded.

In the seventh Commandment, God instructs us not to commit adultery

There had been two weeks of sunny weather, but during the last few days the weather had become very humid and the sky was heavy. It seemed as if the rain would soon come. Mr. Watson was hoping to see some heavy rain because now the grass was a light brown colour and the flowers were drooping, desperate for refreshment. They were not disappointed as within minutes of returning from church, the heavens opened and it poured down. The raindrops were bouncing off the roads and pavements like rubber balls. The drains could hardly collect the water fast enough as the gutters became like rivers. To make it more exciting the downpour was accompanied by thunder and lightning.

"It reminds me of Mount Sinai," remarked Danny. "Earlier this morning I was reading the Commandments and at the end it says the people saw thunder and lightning."

"That's right," responded his father, "but I'm afraid we don't have the mountains smoking as they did."

Lassie did not like storms and found a safe place behind the settee until it had finished.

Throughout dinner the storm continued. As they washed the dishes the doorbell rang and Rachel appeared with raincoat soaked and water pouring off her umbrella.

"You are keen," said Mrs. Watson. "I didn't think you would come in this weather."

"You couldn't keep me away," she replied. "Anyway, it's not very far, I'm pleased to say."

Mrs. Watson took Rachel's coat and umbrella and hung them in the porch to dry. By the time they settled in the lounge the sky had begun to clear and the rain to ease.

"OK, Danny," said Mr. Watson, "you say you have been reading the Commandments so tell us which is the one for today."

"You shall not commit adultery, number seven," he replied, adding the correct number to try and impress the others. "But what does adultery mean?"

"That's a very good question," replied his father. "Before I answer it, can I say that this Commandment is the most difficult to explain to young people like yourselves, but I'll try. Adultery is breaking the marriage vow. Now that is a short, simple answer but let me make it clearer. A husband and wife have a special physical relationship, which expresses their love for one another. From this relationship, children are brought into the world. Adultery is when one of the partners becomes involved in this special relationship with someone else. Am I making myself clear?"

Nods of approval went around the room, which encouraged Mr. Watson to continue.

"I don't want to confuse the subject, but adultery can only be committed when either one or both people concerned are married."

"Many of our friends at school have only one parent and they are very unhappy," said Rachel with a certain amount of concern.

"I'm afraid Rachel, this situation is quite common and one of the main causes of divorce is adultery." added Mr. Watson. "Sadly in many cases, it hurts not only the adults involved but also the children. Unfortunately it is sometimes glamourised in television programmes and books. The result is broken homes, ruined lives, smashed hopes and children separated from one parent or the other. When I was your age if someone had committed adultery it would almost make the headlines, but now if a couple remain together for a lifetime, that is the big news."

"Do we have laws to prevent broken marriages as we have for murder and stealing?" asked Danny.

"Sadly not," replied his father. "The only punishment, if it can be called that, is the divorce court, where the basis of the marriage vow is finally uprooted, but let us now ask what we can learn from this. The first is that the constitution of marriage should be upheld. Jesus certainly approved of it. Someone tell me a story where Jesus attended a wedding."

"I know that one," answered Karen without hesitation. She then began to tell the story of Jesus' visit to the wedding in Cana and how he performed the first miracle by turning water into wine. Her parents were impressed not only by the way the story was told, but also by the way all the events were included.

"...we must never let our desires go above God's law, because adultery not only hurts the partner and children, but it also grieves God. We must remember that all sexual relationships outside of marriage are sinful in God's sight..."

"Can anyone tell me an event when God approved of marriage?" asked Mr. Watson.

Everyone looked blankly at each other and no suggestion came.

"I think I can answer that," replied Mrs. Watson. "In Genesis chapter two, God made Adam and Eve and brought them together as husband and wife. This was the example for all who followed."

"How can we prevent adultery from taking place?" asked Mr. Watson, who then continued to answer his own question. "It is important that we take care over what we see and what we read. Laziness can also lead to this temptation. I know you three are still young, but very soon you may find a girlfriend or boyfriend. Take care over the partner you choose. It is possible to marry a Christian, but for them to be the wrong one. God will guide you if you ask Him and trust Him. Also, remember that their personality and character are far more important than how they look."

"It seems you were fortunate, Dad," said Danny. "With mum you have good on the inside and the outside."

"Thanks Danny, I entirely agree," said Mr. Watson as he gave his wife an affectionate glance. "Could I just add one thing? Be careful how you dress when you get older. Don't try to attract the wrong company."

The discussion continued on subjects that had been raised, but eventually Mr. Watson brought the conversation to a conclusion.

"There are just one or two matters to mention before we break-up. The first is that we must never let our desires go above God's law, because adultery not only hurts the partner and children, but it also grieves God. We must remember that all sexual relationships outside of marriage are sinful in God's sight; so is marriage and sex with two men or two women. One final point I wish to make. There is such a thing as spiritual adultery. Let us never let the love of the world take us from God's presence. We are always tempted to look in other areas for happiness, but there is more than enough in God Himself to satisfy us. God has been faithful, so let us be faithful to Him."

In the eighth Commandment, God instructs us not to steal

It was Saturday morning and Danny had just returned from school after a vigorous game of tennis. He enjoyed the game and always looked forward to meeting his friends on the courts on Saturday. He enjoyed most summer sports, but if he had to choose, his favourite would be cricket. Although he lived in the South of England, he did support his father's county of Yorkshire, though, to be honest, he didn't know why. Perhaps it was his father's influence.

"How long will dinner be Mum, I'm starving?"

"Probably half an hour. Have an apple while you wait. Your father and Karen are in town shopping, but they shouldn't be too long."

Danny sat in a comfortable chair and began to read the local paper that had arrived that morning. After a few minutes, his mother came into the room and noticed that Danny had a serious expression on his face.

"What's the problem?" his mother asked.

Danny didn't reply or move but continued to read.

"You are looking very serious," she said in a louder voice, which made Danny jump with surprise.

"I'm sorry, I didn't realise you were there. I was reading a crime poll in the paper and wasn't aware of the number of break-ins that are taking place. Did you know there has been a break-in along our street?"

"Yes, your father told me about it, although I'm pleased to say no one was hurt and very little was actually taken."

"I'm glad I noticed these before we talk about stealing tomorrow afternoon," said Danny, not quite sure whether he was speaking to himself or his mother.

"Your father and Karen are back and dinner is ready," shouted his mother from the kitchen. Danny didn't need a second invitation.

On Sunday afternoon, Mr. Watson opened his Bible and read the eighth Commandment. He also pointed out that Jesus said in Matthew's Gospel [18] "You shall not steal."

"How would you explain stealing?" he asked.

"Taking another person's money or property without permission," suggested Rachel.

"I couldn't have put it better myself," replied Mr. Watson. "Let me now ask another question. In our talk about an earlier Commandment we discovered that Cain was the first murderer, but can anyone tell me who the first person was to break the eighth Commandment?"

There was an extended pause, but no suggestion came.

"It might surprise you but the first sin committed by a human being was theft. Do you remember in the Garden of Eden, Eve stole the fruit, which did not belong to her? God had clearly told Adam and Eve not to touch it. Just as this was the first sin committed by a human being, it is often the first outward sin committed by children."

"I can remember you telling us not to steal when we were very young," said Karen.

"That's right," replied her father. "This Commandment should be taught to all children from their earliest years."

"If young people were taught all the Commandments, they would grow up into better adults which in turn would make a better country," added Mrs. Watson.

"I was reading a book that was written a number of years ago," said Mr. Watson. "It stated that nearly 75% of all people arrested were charged with some form of robbery. It also told the story of a hotel manageress who revealed that 10,000 coat hangers were stolen from her hotel in 15 years. Another story revealed that 5,000 dresses were stolen from ladies' shops in the West End of London each year."

"That's a lot of hangers and dresses," said Danny with surprise.

"The dresses must have been valuable, but hangers are cheap."

"Danny, in God's sight it is as great a sin to steal a coat hanger as it is to steal a dress," stated his mother.

"I never thought of that," replied Danny.

"When we think of stealing," said Mr. Watson, "we usually think of robbery, mugging, house breaking, shop lifting or similar crimes. The laws of our country cover this Commandment more than any other, there is far more to this one than would appear at first sight. Even respectable people steal, in fact, most people, from time to time, have broken this law."

"Have you dad?" asked Karen wondering if she should have asked such a direct question.

"Yes, I have," admitted her father. "But I try to be more careful now."

"In what way?" asked Karen surprised at the answer given.

"Let's look for a moment at someone who works in an office. How easy it is to take the company's envelopes, stamps and pencils without thinking. What about using the telephone for personal calls and not paying. We can also steal time from our employers by having longer dinner hours or arriving late and leaving early. I know people in my offices that do other work instead of doing what they are paid to do. Even Christians can slip up by doing church work in office hours. I know what I have said does not apply to you just yet, but in a few years it will. Even now you can think of ways you may be breaking this Commandment at school."

They all began to look at other ways of stealing. They looked at advertising which doesn't always tell the truth about what you buy. Also, Mr. Watson mentioned the matter of short weight of products in shops and not paying taxes.

"Actually I can think of something which happens at school occasionally which I think could be classed as stealing but I'm not sure," said Rachel.

"Go on," replied Mr. Watson.

"Well, surely it's a form of stealing to copy someone else's work. I mean aren't we stealing their knowledge, or is that different?"

"I never really thought of that," said Danny slowly, "but it isn't honest is it?"

"No," said his father, "and that is a very good point Rachel. Well done. Now have you ever thought that we can steal from God when we don't spend time with Him each day in prayer and reading His Word. We can also steal from God when we rob Him of His Day or even part of it. I have always tried to make sure that I give a tenth of my income to Christian work. The Bible teaches this and calls it tithing. [19] I know you youngsters do not have much money, but even at your age it is good practice to give a tenth of your pocket money to the work at the church. There are so many ways by which we can rob God."

As the discussion ended, the youngsters left the lounge deep in thought about all that had been said. This pleased Mr. and Mrs. Watson.

In the ninth Commandment, God instructs us not to bear false witness against our neighbour

On the following Thursday afternoon the front door opened and closed within seconds and Karen stormed into the house closely followed by Danny.

"I know she took it!" shouted Karen confidently.

"You did not see her do it," said Danny in a calmer manner.

"It was on my desk last night when we left for home and only Sarah was in the classroom. No one else could have taken it."

"Well you should have put it in your locker or brought it home," suggested Danny.

"Can't we trust people these days to leave what does not belong to them?" Karen replied, still annoyed at the events of the day.

Mrs. Watson was preparing the evening meal when she heard the front door close a good deal louder than usual. She dried her hands and made her way to the front room where Danny and Karen were still in conversation.

"Hold it! What's the problem? You sound like you've lost ten pounds and only found one."

"Mum, you remember that new pen and pencil set that Gran'dad gave me for my birthday? Well, I'm sure Sarah must have taken it because it was not on my desk this morning and she was the last out of the classroom on Wednesday night."

"Have you proof?" asked her mother.

"Well, no, but it couldn't have been anyone else."

"You are making a judgement without knowing the facts. Have you said anything to Sarah or your teacher?"

"Sarah said she did not see it, and our teacher will not be back until tomorrow."

"Well, go to your teacher first thing in the morning and ask her if it has been handed in."

With that, the conversation finished, but Karen was very unhappy and quiet all evening.

The following afternoon, Karen returned from school a little shame-faced.

"Well, any news?" asked her mother.

Karen then began to tell her mother how one of the cleaners saw the pencil case and put it in the teacher's desk for safety.

"I almost felt I should apologise to Sarah," said Karen.

"It seems a coincidence that on Sunday we discuss 'you shall not bear false witness'. When we consider it, I think we will see the need to be sure of the facts before we put the blame on someone else."

Everyone was so pleased after last Sunday's downpour, to be seated in the garden with the warm sun beating down on their heads. Mrs. Watson had just brought out a tray of drinks and settled into the chair that had been reserved for her.

"Also remember," said Mrs. Watson, "that exaggeration, with the intention of impressing those who hear us, is a form of lying. When people find out that you exaggerate, they will never believe you or even want to listen to you again."

"Are you all sitting comfortably?" asked Mr. Watson. "Then, I'll begin."

"I've heard that somewhere before," said Danny.

Mr. Watson continued, "You will notice that with many Commandments, they are repeated word for word in the New

Testament by Jesus. In Matthew's Gospel, chapter 19 and verse 18, Jesus told the rich, young ruler that he must not bear false witness. There are two words in the law of the land, which describe the breaking of this Commandment. The first is perjury. Don't charge for the dictionary, as I will try to explain. Perjury is when a witness in a law court intentionally makes a statement which he knows is untrue. Often people who are accused of crime tell untruths to gain freedom. The second word is libel, which means that a person cannot publish an untrue statement against someone else. Now, why do people tell lies about others?"

"To cover their own sins," suggested Rachel.

"That can be true," confirmed Mr. Watson. "Any other ideas?"

"When we don't know all the facts," said Karen, remembering the events of last week.

"There is another reason why people tell untruths about others and that is to impress their listeners."

"We are back to the tongue again," remarked Karen.

"That's right," said her father. "Telling lies either by speaking or writing is bearing false witness. It all comes down to the importance of the truth. We are constantly communicating with each other, so it is essential that the truth is protected, if not we will injure someone's reputation."

"Also remember," said Mrs. Watson, "that exaggeration, with the intention of impressing those who hear us, is a form of lying. When people find out that you exaggerate, they will never believe you or even want to listen to you again."

"I suppose boasting can be a form of lying," suggested Karen.

"It can certainly lead to it," replied Mr. Watson, "which should show us how wise God is. We have two defences against the tongue which are our teeth and our lips."

"I like that," said Danny thoughtfully.

"There is a verse in Zechariah [20], Mr. Watson reminded them, "which commands us to speak the truth to our neighbour at all times.

The danger in lying is that we usually need to tell more lies to cover up the first. Also, lying can develop quickly into committing other sins."

General conversation continued for quite a while, but Danny remained silent, yet very thoughtful.

"Any problems?" asked his father.

"Not really," Danny answered hesitatingly. "I was just wondering what the position would be if I told an untruth because wrong information had been given to me."

"I'm glad you mentioned that," said his father. "Every falsehood is not a lie. There are times when we have been given information and sincerely believe that we are stating facts. If we have no intention of misleading others, then it cannot be a deliberate lie."

Mr. Watson noticed relief spread across Danny's face, but did not ask any questions.

"We will need to finish soon," continued Mr. Watson, "but there is just one other point I would like to share. How can we protect ourselves from being a false witness? The first is to avoid the company of gossips. In other words, don't get involved with other people's affairs. We have a big enough task in looking after our own. Secondly, remember our own weaknesses. Often we see a small fault in someone else, when we have many more of our own. Finally, if others speak badly about you, God knows the truth, so don't worry what they say."

There was a short pause to consider what had been said, and then Mrs. Watson called all hands to the kitchen to help with the tea.

In the tenth Commandment, God instructs us not to covet

Another week had quickly passed and the Watsons were tucking into their Sunday lunch. "Have you seen our neighbour's new car?" asked Mrs. Watson to her husband as he was enjoying his rhubarb crumble.

"Is that just an observation, or...?" he replied, swallowing his last mouthful.

"Yes dear, just an observation," said Mrs. Watson, suddenly aware of the title of the final Commandment.

"Make the coffee please, Karen," said her father. "We have much to discuss this afternoon and I would like to start as soon as Rachel arrives."

He had hardly uttered the words before the doorbell rang and it was not long before they were enjoying their drinks in the lounge, ready for Mr. Watson to begin.

"Well, we have been meeting like this for the past eleven weeks and we come to the tenth and final Commandment. I hope you have learnt as much as I have. One lesson I have been taught is how God provides for our security and well being, particularly in the last four Commandments. Have you noticed how he provides protection for ourselves in the sixth Commandment; He gives protection for the family in the seventh; for the safety of property in the eighth and for our reputation in the ninth. God not only prevents outward crimes, but also inward desires. Now that leads me to ask the question, what does 'covet' mean?"

Danny looked at the notepad in front of him and said confidently, "It means to desperately want what belongs to someone else."

"That's a good definition, where did you think of that?" his father asked in surprise.

Danny felt that he had to be honest after last Sunday's discussion. "I looked it up in the dictionary," he said with tongue in cheek.

"I hope you will note that in Luke's Gospel [21], Jesus warns people about being careful of covetousness," said Mr. Watson. "Even Paul in the letter to Romans [22] said that they were not to covet."

"Do we have a law against it like we do with stealing, murder and those two difficult words we used last week?" asked Karen. "I'm afraid I have forgotten them."

"You mean perjury and libel," said her mother trying to help.

"That's it. I knew what they meant but I couldn't remember the words."

"Don't worry," assured her father. "There are no laws against covetousness because it involves a state of mind. I don't want to make it difficult, but the mind covers will power, morals, thoughts, intentions and desires. But remember that covetous thoughts can develop into action, such as adultery and theft."

"I suppose we all covet in our minds," suggested Rachel. "A friend of mine had a new bicycle for her birthday and I immediately wished it was mine."

> " Coveting is letting the world get into our heart. We live in the world, but the world should not live in us. It's like water which is useful for sailing a ship, but the danger comes when water gets into the ship."

"I fell into that trap before you came," acknowledged Mrs. Watson. "When I saw our neighbour's car, I was a little envious when I looked at ours."

"Most people are in the same position," said Mr. Watson. "Whether it's a larger house, better car, bigger salary or more pocket money, we desire more when we see what other people have. Also remember that the more you have, the more you want."

"The big question is whether people are happier and more

contented with having more," suggested Mrs. Watson. "The problem with human nature is that we are never satisfied. We are always trying to keep up with the Jones's."

"Who are they?" asked Karen.

"Nobody in particular," her mother replied. "It's just an expression, meaning that if someone you know has something appealing, you must have the same. People are so greedy for more, yet what we are short of is contentment with what we already possess."

"Your mother is correct," confirmed Mr. Watson. "All I hear is 'I want', or 'give me!' We never seem to ask, 'Do I need?' Coveting and greediness cannot be separated."

"The human head is quite small compared to the rest of the body," said Mrs. Watson.

"That's debatable with some people I know," said Karen laughing. Karen had a very infectious laugh and once she started it was difficult not to join in. Eventually Mr. Watson managed to gain control and asked his wife to continue.

"What I was trying to say was that the head contains what can be the most dangerous parts of the body which can lead to temptation. The tongue, the ears and the eyes, and it is the latter that gives us the desire to covet."

Mr. Watson then went on to explain that there are four steps to coveting. The first step begins with an evil thought. The second step is when that evil thought stays in the mind and we even begin to enjoy it. The third step is when we give it our approval and the final step is when we commit the act. He continued by quoting the words of Jesus in Matthew's Gospel [23] when He said that out of the heart come evil thoughts, murders and adulteries, and Jesus put evil thoughts first.

Danny was writing as fast as he could to get those four points down on his notepad.

"What people forget," said Mrs. Watson, "is that they will not live on this earth for ever. The Bible tells us that our life does not consist of the things we possess. We come into this world with nothing and we go out of this world the same way. We cannot take our money and property with us."

"What we need is contentment," suggested Mr. Watson. "It's the best way to keep people from breaking this final Commandment."

"I think it was wise of God to put this as the last one," said Rachel.

"That's right," agreed Mr. Watson. "It's like a fence or wall to protect the rest. Coveting is letting the world get into our heart. We live in the world, but the world should not live in us. It's like water which is useful for sailing a ship, but the danger comes when water gets into the ship."

"I like that," said Danny, again writing as fast as possible to get it down in his notepad.

Suddenly there was a knock at the door.

"I'll get it!" shouted Karen, jumping to her feet.

"I'm not expecting anyone," said Mrs. Watson, wondering who the caller could be.

"It's Rachel's father."

"Show him in," said Mr. Watson as he rose from the chair and made his way to the door.

"Pleased to meet you," he said grasping Mr. Rowland's hand firmly. "Don't worry about the dog, she is very friendly despite her loud barking." Lassie always charged to the door when anyone came in.

"I'm sorry to disturb your discussion, but we've just heard that my mother has been taken ill, and we're going to see her as soon as possible."

"We are sorry to hear that," said Mrs. Watson. "We had nearly finished anyway, so there's no need to apologise. I hope things are not as bad as they sound."

As Mr. Rowland and Rachel were leaving, Mr. Rowland turned back as though he had forgotten something.

"I just wanted to thank you for having Rachel these past few Sundays. She has told us all about your discussions and it has made us think about what has been said."

"It's been our pleasure," said Mr. Watson.

"Before you go, what about coming with your wife for tea next Sunday?" asked Mrs. Watson. "You would be most welcome."

"That's very kind of you," said Mr. Rowland. "We would be very pleased to come."

"Rachel can come at around two as usual and we can have tea at five," suggested Mrs. Watson.

Mr. Rowland and Rachel hurried to their car and were soon driving away.

A lesson is learned

"How is your grandma?" asked Mrs. Watson as Rachel arrived the following Sunday afternoon. "She's a little better, thank you. My parents have been with her most of the time and the doctor says she should make a complete recovery if she takes care over the next few days."

"That's good news. We are looking forward to your parents joining us for tea."

Mrs. Watson and Rachel made their way into the lounge. All the family were pleased that Rachel had brought good news regarding her grandma.

"Well, we must begin as soon as possible, so that we can all help with the tea before Rachel's parents arrive," suggested Mrs. Watson.

As soon as the empty coffee cups were taken into the kitchen, Mr. Watson began by giving a short summary of each Commandment and explaining that we would live in a better world if they were kept and respected.

"The law is important in every area of life," continued Mr. Watson. "You must have rules and regulations at school or else the result would be chaos, and I don't think that would please your teacher. I think we can answer Mr. Dobson's claim."

They all agreed that the world would be a better place if people obeyed the Commandments.

"You see, they and the whole Bible are our Creator's

instructions so that we can live as God intended. If I bought your mother a dish washer..."

"I wish you would," interrupted Danny with a grin.

"...I would hope she would read the manufacturer's instructions. Now we are wonderfully made and our minds and bodies need constant care. In the Bible, God has told us how we should care for them. They are His instructions."

Mr. Watson then continued to explain that because we are born with a tendency to sin and live in sin, we couldn't keep God's Law perfectly. Because of our failure to do this, we face God's judgement.

"What do you mean when you say we are born sinners?" asked Rachel.

"When we are born into the world we have a sinful nature. We might look innocent in our mother's arms but when we begin to talk we soon learn to say 'I shan't', 'I can't' and 'I won't'. If parents doubt whether their children are born sinners I usually ask them if they ever had to teach their children to be naughty. The answer is always, No! The most difficult task for parents is to bring up their children to be good decent citizens."

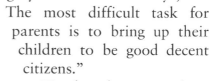

He then began to show how Jesus, who is God's Son made man, kept the law perfectly, because He had no sin. He died upon the cross in the sinners' place so that we could be forgiven. Instead of God's judgement we can have His mercy and forgiveness.

"I suppose it's something like us," suggested Karen. "If

we do wrong we are punished, but because you love us we are forgiven if we are really sorry."

"That's right," said Mr. Watson, "although it is more than being sorry with God. The Bible uses the word 'repentance' which means a change of life and direction."

"If Jesus forgives us, why are God's Commandments important?" asked Rachel.

"I was reading Psalm 19 this morning," replied Mr. Watson," in verse 7 it tells us that God's Law is perfect, and is there to bring us to repentance. How do we know that sin dwells in us? We know because of our failure to keep God's Law. If there is no law, we will have no sense of sin. If we have no sense of sin, then we have no need of Jesus to save us from our sins.

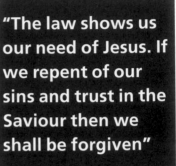

"The law shows us our need of Jesus. If we repent of our sins and trust in the Saviour then we shall be forgiven"

The cross and heaven will have no meaning and we would be without hope."

Mr. Watson then went on to explain more fully that the Ten Commandments and the good news of Jesus cannot be separated as one leads to the other. The law shows us our need of Jesus. If we repent of our sins and trust in the Saviour then we shall be forgiven.

Mr. Watson glanced at the clock on the mantlepiece. "Look it's nearly half past four. All hands on deck!"

In no time the table was set and the tea ready. At exactly five o'clock, the doorbell rang and Mr. Rowland introduced his wife to the Watsons. After a brief chat in the lounge, Mr. Watson asked everyone if they would take their places. The lovely spread was enjoyed by all. When the meal was finished, the youngsters were asked to clear the dishes and make themselves useful while the adults continued their conversation.

"It's been good to meet you," said Mrs. Watson.

"Last Sunday I said we had learned a great deal from Rachel due to her visits here," acknowledged Mr. Rowland. "That's true, but we have also realised how we could have helped her more. We have provided food and clothing and acted like a moral policeman, but our home has been nothing more than a filling station for the day and a parking place at night. From what Rachel has been saying to us, we have realised that spiritual values have been neglected. We have sent Rachel to Sunday school, but we should have taken her."

"What my husband is trying to say," said Mrs. Rowland, "is that we have had to learn a lesson, and through your help, Rachel has taught us to think again about the Ten Commandments."

"Well, following this afternoon's discussion, she might have something more important to tell you," said Mr. Watson. "Why don't you come along to church with us this evening? It would please Rachel very much if both our families went together."

"We would love to," admitted Mrs. Rowland.

"Rachel!" exclaimed Mr. Rowland.

Rachel came into the lounge with her hands and arms covered in soapsuds. Karen stood by the door with the tea towel. Evidently Danny had done a good job in supervising.

"We are coming to church with you tonight," continued Mr. Rowland.

Rachel ran and put both arms around her parents.

"I'm so pleased, I hoped you would."

After supper, Danny and Karen had gone to their rooms for the night, which left Mr. and Mrs. Watson by themselves, with Lassie stretched out at their feet.

"It has been a good day."

"Yes," agreed her husband. "Mr. Dobson has been proved wrong. We have living proof that the Ten Commandments are relevant today."

Chapter 13

References

1, Exodus 20:1, 31:18, Deuteronomy 10:4-5

2, James 2:10

3, Matthew 22:37

4, Mark 12:30

5, Luke 10:27

6, Genesis 2:2-3

7, Acts 20:7, 1 Corinthians 16:2

8, Genesis 46:29

9, 1 Kings 2:1

10, Proverbs 6:20

11, Matthew 15:4

12, Luke 2:51

13, Colossians 3:20

14, 1 Timothy 5:16

15, Matthew 5:21-22

16, Deuteronomy 19:5

17, 2 Samuel 11:15

18, Matthew 19:18

19, Malachi 3:8-10

20, Zechariah 8:16

21, Luke 12:15

22, Romans 7:7

23, Matthew 15:19

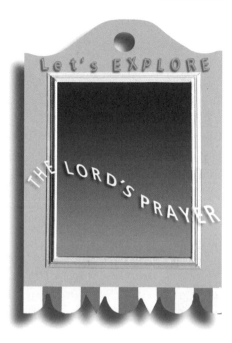

Prayer is important

D anny sat thoughtfully in the armchair with his hands clasped around his knees, gently swaying backwards and forwards. His mother was usually at home when he returned from school—but not this afternoon. She had received an urgent call from an elderly lady who lived on the other side of town and as she was the only district nurse on call, she had to attend.

Danny didn't hear the front door open or his mother enter the room.

"Hey! Wake up, you seem miles away."

With a jump he came back to the real world again. He then realised he had been sitting for nearly half an hour concerned about his friend.

"What's the problem?" asked his mother.

"Oh, I'm just worried about my friend Justin."

"Can I help?" she asked

"Not really… well perhaps you can…" he said with a little hesitation. As they were talking, Lassie came into the room and sensing Danny was not his usual self, lay down beside him with her chin resting across his foot. Danny paused to stroke her head.

"There are a small group of lads at school who are always in trouble; some of us think they are taking drugs. Well, Justin is now being bullied because he won't join them. We know taking drugs is wrong and dangerous, but…"

"Do they bully you?" asked his mother.

"No, I'm too big, but Justin is short and quiet, so they pick on him."

"We'll have a chat with your father when he gets home, but try and support Justin as much as you can, and pray about it."

"I do, but I don't seem to be getting any help even though I'm asking for it," replied Danny.

"Look Danny, prayer isn't easy," acknowledged his mother. "But we must pray even when we don't feel like doing it. God does hear us."

"But you and dad seem to find it so easy and you hardly ever seem to have problems or get worried about things or people."

"It's perhaps that we don't show it, but I can assure you that we have our difficulties like everyone else. Shall we have a chat with your father about it when he comes home, he shouldn't be long now?" suggested his mother, glancing at the clock on the wall. Danny nodded in agreement but remained silent.

It wasn't long before Karen arrived home, bouncing through the door full of life. She had been taking part in a hockey match, hoping eventually to play in the school team.

"Hi everyone!"

Only her mother acknowledged the greeting. Danny still sat deep in thought.

"Who's looking miserable then? Come on, cheer up, it's not the end of the world."

Danny either chose to ignore her remarks or else he was so deep in thought that he hadn't heard Karen speak to him.

At six o'clock the family was complete. Mr Watson had returned from the office, thankful to be away from the rush and noise of city traffic. As he went upstairs to change into more casual clothes, Mrs Watson took the opportunity of telling him about her conversation with Danny and suggested that after dinner they have a chat together.

By the time Mr Watson had

come downstairs, Danny was much brighter, and deep in conversation with his sister on a subject that was clearly just between the two of them. They often discussed issues together, even though it did sometimes end in strong disagreements.

"Dinner's almost ready!" shouted Mrs Watson from the kitchen. "Can you set the table please Karen?"

"I'm coming."

Danny was always ready for his meals for he had a huge appetite. His father said he had one meal a day, which began at eight in the morning and finished at eight in the evening. It was surprising that he didn't put on weight. This annoyed his father who was always dieting to keep his weight down.

After dinner was over, Danny suggested taking Lassie for a walk before it was too dark. As soon as the word 'walk' was mentioned, Lassie jumped to her feet with great excitement, wagging her tail wildly and looking round for her lead.

"Do you mind if I join you?" asked his father. "It was so stuffy in the office today with the heating on and windows closed. Some fresh air would be most welcome."

It was now autumn and the evening was quite chilly so both wrapped up to keep warm. The walk gave Mr Watson the opportunity to talk with Danny who welcomed a sympathetic ear.

The Watsons lived very close to a large park through which a river flowed. It was a pleasant sight to see the mallards, Canadian geese and moorhens swimming downstream. Lassie had ample room to enjoy herself, especially if it meant chasing squirrels.

"I think it's time to make our way home. Call the dog, Danny, that's if she has any energy left."

It wasn't long before they arrived home to a warm house.

"Had a good time?" asked Karen as they entered the room. "These men are very good at finding things to do when washing up needs to be done."

"We'll get the supper ready," said Danny, knowing that would not be too difficult.

"Are you sure you can manage it?" replied Karen.

"That's enough," said her mother. "Come on, let's see you both get down to some homework."

Soon the twins were seated at the table with their study books covering every square inch that was available. They often did their homework together, especially when exams were drawing near. This gave them an opportunity to question each other on difficult subjects.

Mr Watson settled on one side of the fireplace with a book in his hands, while his wife curled up on the settee with the crossword from the daily newspaper.

It was quiet for some time with every member of the family involved in their task, when suddenly Danny broke the silence.

"Mum, when we were out with the dog, I was talking to dad about Justin and he said that if Justin agreed, he would go and talk to his parents about it."

"We also talked about prayer and dad suggested we discuss it on Sunday afternoons."

"Prayer is a very

important subject," he said. "I was wondering if it would be helpful to us all if we could discuss the greatest prayer ever uttered. I was thinking of the Lord's Prayer, as it has so much to say to us."

"That would be great," agreed Karen. "Can Rachel come again?"

"I can't see why not," replied her mother.

"Can I ring her now?"

"Just a minute," interrupted her father. "We should first decide when to begin."

"This Sunday," suggested Danny enthusiastically. "Anyway, you always tell us to strike while the iron is hot."

"True, but give me time to put the plug in."

Eventually the family agreed to begin next week, and decided to divide the Lord's Prayer so they had a different theme for each Sunday.

"Can I ring Rachel now?" asked Karen impatiently.

"Go on," said her mother. "We won't have any peace until you have done so and don't talk for too long as you still have homework to finish."

"Won't be long, promise."

Within minutes Karen was back with a smile on her face, assuring the family that all arrangements had been made and Rachel was looking forward to coming.

Teach me how to Pray

Saturday was usually a busy day for the whole family and today was no exception. Mr Watson had decided it would be a good idea to turn the attic into a fourth bedroom for when they had visitors. For the last few weeks the joiners had been very busy and the work was finally complete. All it needed was some wallpaper and paint. Fortunately, Mrs Watson enjoyed papering and Mr Watson liked painting. They had been to the shops early this Saturday and chosen their colour scheme and paper. All it needed now was putting on the walls. Although it would take longer than one day to finish, they made a good start and both felt pleased with the work they had done.

Danny and Karen were rather glad to be out of the way but wished they were doing something better than revising for their exams. However, they both knew it was necessary if they wanted to get good marks.

By the time Sunday came round they were all thankful for the opportunity of resting their bodies and minds, although Mr Watson would see to it that their minds were not completely at rest as he had prepared some questions for the afternoon's discussion.

Rachel was now a welcome member of the family and looked forward to these Sunday afternoons. She arrived in good time and it wasn't long before Mr Watson was introducing the subject of the Lord's Prayer.

"Before we look at the Lord's Prayer itself, let's think about the importance of prayer generally."

During the past few evenings he had been thinking of this discussion and wanted all the others to join in.

"My first question may seem very simple, but what is prayer?"

It was an easy question, but at first no replies were made until Karen attempted to answer.

"To me, prayer is sharing our experiences with God. He hears our problems, as well as our thanks for all the good things He has given us. We also bring our requests to Him."

"That's a good start," he assured her. "Some people only come to pray when difficulties come their way. Unfortunately, they forget God when things are going well. I remember on one occasion travelling by air when an engine failed. People began to pray who afterwards admitted they had never prayed before. We landed safely, but I wonder how many thanked God for a safe landing."

"I was just thinking of a verse in Romans," said Mrs Watson. "It says that we cannot pray properly to someone we believe does not exist."

"That's right." acknowledged Mr Watson.

"We will look at your reply, Karen, in more detail as the weeks go by, but first of all we acknowledge that prayer is talking to someone who exists and has power to answer our requests."

Mr Watson then moved on to a second question, asking why we pray only to God. Everyone admitted that although the question seemed easy, you had to think very carefully before answering.

> We need to remember that God has three ways of answering our requests. The first is 'yes', the second is 'no' and the third is 'not yet'. So when we do not receive an answer immediately we must show patience, as the time may not be right."

"I suppose because only God hears our prayer," replied Rachel with some hesitation. She wasn't sure why she took so long to answer, as it seemed obvious.

"Any other suggestions?" asked Mr Watson.

"Because only God can help," said Danny, still wondering why God didn't seem to be helping him even when he asked for it. But, thought Danny, perhaps God was helping him and he wasn't aware of it.

Mr Watson then began to explain how important it was to pray for things that would please God. Sometimes we pray in a selfish way and God doesn't answer because it isn't good for us. He told them how when he left school he prayed to be rich, with a big car and a large house and good health to enjoy them. When God didn't answer, he eventually realised that he should be trying to please Him and put Him first before all these things.

"Do you find it hard to pray?" asked Rachel.

"Sometimes I do," admitted Mrs Watson. "When I was very young I was told to use my hand as a visual aid. When we pray with our hands together, the thumb is the nearest to me. This reminded me to pray for my family and friends. The first finger is normally used for pointing and showing people the way to go. I then prayed for our minister and teachers who guide us in the right direction. My second finger is the longest and most important. This tells me to pray for the important people such as our leaders both in this country and overseas. My third finger is the weakest. It can do very little unless the others help. This reminds me to pray for those who are ill, hungry and homeless, in fact, all who are less fortunate than myself. Finally my little finger reminds me to pray for myself. God should always be first, others second and ourselves last."

All the family listened carefully with interest and then again went through each finger trying to remember the points, which Mrs Watson had made.

"I hope that may have helped," said Mrs Watson.

"Yes, it has," replied Rachel.

"When you get older your prayers will extend further but that may help you to begin."

"Can I just share another thought which may help?" continued Mr Watson. "Sometimes we expect God to answer in a way that suits us. We need to remember that God has three ways of answering our requests. The first is 'yes', the second is 'no' and the third is 'not yet'. So when we do not receive an answer immediately we must show patience, as the time may not be right."

As Mr Watson looked through his list of questions, he realised that most had been answered already but one or two had not been fully explained.

"We haven't thought yet of the different ways we can pray. Any suggestions?"

"We can pray by ourselves as we do in our Quiet-time," said Karen.

"We can pray with other Christians as we do at church," suggested Danny.

"What about praying as a family? We do this now," joined in Rachel, encouraged that her parents had recently started going to church regularly.

Mrs Watson reminded them that prayer need not be spoken out loud. Even at school or work we can pray quietly. She often asked God to help her as she travelled in her work throughout the district.

The afternoon had passed quickly and Mr Watson briefly went over the points they had raised before tea was prepared.

When he had finished Danny suggested that the best way of ending the afternoon was in prayer.

Mr Watson gladly agreed to that request.

The family comes to stay

Last week had been full of activity. Mrs Watson's sister and her husband had brought their three children, Peter, Diane and Wendy, to stay for a few days during the school half term. Although the extra bedroom was not quite finished they had been able to make it comfortable for them. Wendy was the youngest of the family and had been fostered at an early age by Mr and Mrs Marshall. They were hoping that quite soon they would be able to adopt her as one their own children. They were all younger than Danny and Karen, but they got on very well together. Lassie was delighted to have new friends to play with.

The weather had been good during their stay, so in the daytime they were able to enjoy being outside. After dinner various board games were played, with the adults sometimes joining in. Their favourite was Bible Challenge, although some questions were too difficult even for the adults. Lassie was usually worn out by evening and curled up by the fire quite contented.

On the Saturday, the house began to return to near normal and by the evening everything seemed neat and tidy ready for the following day.

On most Sundays, Rachel came to the Watsons' after dinner, but sometimes, as today, she came back after the morning service to have dinner with them. Mrs Watson always seemed well organised in the home and made sure everyone played their part in helping to clear the dishes. Soon they were sitting in their usual places ready for the session to begin.

"How does the Lord's Prayer start?" asked Mr Watson.

"Our Father, in heaven," answered Karen with confidence.

"That's right, but can you tell me what comes exactly before that?" he continued.

There was silence with puzzled faces around the room.

"Well, if you find Matthew's Gospel, Chapter six and verse nine, you will find that Jesus begins by telling the disciples the way they should pray. The Ten Commandments are the rule of our life, and the Lord's Prayer is an example of how we should pray."

Mr Watson then went on to emphasise that Jesus said, "After this manner, or example, we should pray." He tried to show that the Lord's prayer was a very good guideline, because it was given by its author. That is why it is called the Lord's Prayer. The Ten Commandments were written by God's finger and now the Lord's Prayer is spoken by God's Son.

"When I was thinking of this prayer," said Mrs Watson, "I realised how short it was. A great amount has been said in few words and yet it contains everything."

"And most of it I understand," added Rachel, "apart from one or two difficult parts."

"Well let's look at the pattern or model," suggested Mr Watson. "First of all, who was this prayer a model for, everyone or just His disciples?"

"It must be His disciples," replied Karen, 'because only His followers can call God their Father."

"Can anyone add to that?"

"Well," said Danny, "our minister once said that God made us all, but He can only be our Father when we are His children, and we come into the family when we become Christians."

"That's right," replied his father, pleased that Danny had listened carefully to the minister's messages.

"I suppose your cousin Wendy is a good example," added Mrs Watson. "When she is adopted into the family, she will be your auntie and uncle's daughter, or their child. She will be part of the family and call her adopted parents mother and father. So when we come into God's family as Christians, we can call God our Father, and He is the best of all."

"That leads immediately to the question, why?" asked Mr Watson.

"Because He loves us the most," answered Rachel. "Somewhere in the Bible it says 'God is love,'[1] Our earthly parents love us very much, but God loves us even more."

"Has anyone any other reasons why they think God is the best Father?"

"Because He knows everything," replied Danny. "He knows what we need, and what is best for us."

"He always listens to us," added Karen. "He is never too busy or too tired."

"Can I just add two more reasons that have come to mind?" asked Mrs Watson. "God is perfect, which is unlike our earthly parents, even though they do their best. Also, God never dies. Our mothers and fathers do, but God lives for ever."

"I didn't think of that," said Karen honestly.

"Neither did I," admitted her father.

They continued to talk about God's concern for them as his children and how He wants the best for them. Then Mrs Watson changed the conversation by asking how we should respond to God as His children.

"We should always try to please Him." replied Rachel.

"Yes, but how?"

"By not doing wrong things on purpose," suggested Danny knowing that they were all guilty of this.

"You were right in saying that, but now think of positive things."

Mr Watson was pleased to let his wife guide the youngsters' thoughts.

"When we help people such as the elderly and sick, especially those in hospital," said Karen who enjoyed doing those things.

"We should please Him by trying to be like Him," added Rachel

"I thought you had fallen asleep, Dad," said Danny realising that his father had not spoken for some time.

"I'm listening, don't worry."

Mrs Watson was reminded of Peter, her nephew, when he was very young. She told them how he always wanted to be like his father. He copied him in nearly everything, even in trying to shave until his mother caught him using the electric razor. He wanted to be like his father because he loved and respected him.

They continued a little longer until Mr Watson said they should finish, and do one other thing that would please God.

"I think I know what you mean," said Karen. "We should go to church, to worship Him and thank Him for being our Heavenly Father."

"Well done," replied her father, very pleased with their response.

Bonfire night at the farm

The Watsons were enjoying their evening meal when the telephone rang. "I'll get it!" Mrs Watson picked up the receiver and told everyone it was her sister, Pam.

That was the signal to put Mum's dinner in the oven as it was likely to be a long call. Pam and Tony lived on a farm one hour's drive away, so Karen and Danny often spent part of their holiday helping, especially during the summer.

"Pam wants to know if we would like to go and spend bonfire-night with them?" asked Mrs Watson. "They're inviting friends from the church and arranging a barbecue."

"Not half," said Danny excitedly.

Mrs Watson thought this would give the twins something to look forward to.

It wasn't long before Saturday came and they were making their way to Clayton Farm. They arrived in good time so that Danny and Karen could help Uncle Tony with the cows.

Other friends began to arrive and by half past six, the farmyard was full of cars with people greeting each other. There were many young people about the twins' age, so nobody felt by themselves.

It was a clear evening, although quite cool so everyone was well wrapped up. Mr Watson noticed that Danny was looking at the stars and seemed to be dreaming.

"You look a million miles away, Danny. What are you thinking about?"

Danny, still looking thoughtful, said "I was just thinking how powerful God must be to make this earth and all the stars and keep them in place. The Bible says He made them out of nothing and I find it difficult to understand, but I know it is true."

"Yes, Danny," replied his father. "We are not meant to understand, or we should be as powerful as God, and that can never be. The important thing is to thank Him for making the world and putting us in it. Remember that He is always ready to hear us when we pray to Him."

"I know that, Dad."

Just then, Uncle Tony shouted to everyone, "The bonfire will be lit in five minutes!"

A stream of people, all ages, made their way round the back of the farm buildings where the bonfire was standing. Soon it was blazing merrily, sending out welcome heat.

Uncle Tony had said that he would supply the fireworks, as he wanted to make sure the animals were not frightened by sudden noises. Everyone chatted away happily enjoying the colourful sight.

As the bonfire died down, Uncle Tony pointed to where the barbecue was being prepared. Mrs Watson and her sister had been busy cooking hot dogs, baked potatoes and burgers so it wasn't long before the smell of the food tempted everyone to tuck in.

> "We hallow or respect God's Name because of our gratitude to Him for all He has done for us, particularly for sending His Son to die for our sins that they might be forgiven."

Danny was so full he could hardly walk back to the car, and as they returned home the family agreed that it had been a great evening.

After the busy Saturday, it was good to have a quiet Sunday and Karen looked forward to telling Rachel about the bonfire in the afternoon and fireworks.

Rachel arrived just after two o'clock, in time for a cup of coffee. It had been another cold day so warm drinks were most welcome.

"I think we've all finished drinking our coffees, so let's look at another area of the Lord's Prayer." suggested Mr Watson. "Last week we discussed God being our Father, so this afternoon we should consider the phrase that follows, which is 'Hallowed be your Name'. What does hallowed mean?"

"I think it means holy," said Rachel with hesitation.

"Yes, that's right. It means to set apart and to use the name with great respect. His Name is very special."

"We talked about this when we looked at the Commandments last summer," said Karen, pleased that her memory had not failed her.

"But which Commandment?" asked her father.

Probably my memory isn't too good after all, thought Karen, as she tried to remember if it was the second or third. Eventually she suggested the third and was pleased when her father assured her she had answered correctly.

"When we hallow God's Name, we are also glorifying it," suggested Mrs Watson. "This means that we must speak highly of Him and only think or speak of Him with the greatest respect. The writers in the Old Testament, particularly the Psalms, took great care in using God's Name. This must be an example to us today."

"That's right," said Mr Watson. "We give respect to God's Name because of His goodness, wisdom, power, faithfulness, and holiness."

"When we have finished the Lord's Prayer could we discuss the different parts of God's character?" asked Danny.

"Hold on, Danny," replied his father. "Sometime we might do that, but we must not wander from today's subject."

Danny thought his suggestion so good that he made a note of it in his pad so it would not be forgotten.

"Your mother, a few minutes ago, mentioned the writers in the Old Testament having respect for God's Name. Well, in those days a name was not generally regarded as a title to separate one person from another. It really expressed the nature of the person. So if a person changed in any way, a new name was given and this name was linked with the person. Can you think of people in the Bible whose names were changed?"

"Well there was Abram and Sarai," said Karen quickly, before anyone else thought of those two.

"Very good." replied her mother.

"There was Jacob who became Israel," said Danny.

"Can you think of someone in the New Testament?" asked Mrs Watson.

During the silence, Rachel didn't want to be left out, yet she couldn't think of anyone.

"Yes!" she shouted suddenly. "Paul became Saul, or was it the other way round?"

"You have the names right, but it was Saul who became Paul," replied Mrs Watson. "After his conversion his name was changed."

"Now if people's names show something of their character, this also applies to God," said Mr Watson.

With his help there was much rustling of paper as they eagerly searched through their Bibles to find the names given to God.

"When we suggested people whose names were changed," commented Rachel, "We forgot Jesus because He had many different names."

"That's right," replied Mr Watson "he had a number of titles, such as 'Emmanuel' which means 'God is with us', and 'Messiah'.

The conversation had drifted a little and, as they needed to finish quickly, Mr Watson brought them back to the main part of their discussion.

"We hallow or respect God's Name because, as the chorus tells us, 'His Name is higher than any other'. We also do it because of our gratitude to Him for all He has done for us, particularly for sending His Son to die for our sins that they might be forgiven."

"We can also glorify God when we see the sky, especially at night with so many stars," said Rachel.

Danny and his father looked at one another and smiled as they remembered their conversation at the barbecue the previous evening.

"We can praise God when we see the beauty of the rainbow, the hills and the sea," added Danny thinking of the many holidays they had spent at the coast.

"I can glorify God when I study biology and think of the human body," joined in Karen.

"Yes" said her mother, "and just remember that when God made man, he succeeded first time and didn't need many attempts as scientists do today. God has been good to us in giving more than we deserve. It just proves that those who misuse His Name do not know Him."

"We have thought of God's Name both in the Commandments and now in the Lord's Prayer." said Mr Watson. "Let us make sure that we respect it in all we say, think and do. The glory of God is the first thing we should desire."

Danny has an accident

It was Tuesday evening and Mrs Watson was preparing the vegetables for the evening meal. Karen had been home for more than an hour, but there was no sign of Danny.

"I hope he's all right," said Mrs Watson. "He's not usually as late as this, unless he tells me the previous day that he has to stay longer at school."

"He'll be fine," assured Karen, but also inwardly she wondered what was keeping him so late.

"Mrs Watson rushed from the kitchen, lifted up the receiver and her face went pale..."

As they were talking, the telephone rang. Mrs Watson rushed from the kitchen, lifted up the receiver and her face went pale.

"What's the matter?" asked Karen when her mother put the telephone down.

"It's Danny."

"What's happened?"

"A car had to swerve to avoid someone and caught Danny's bike. They don't think it's serious, but he's been taken to hospital."

"What are you going to do?" asked Karen.

"It's too late to ring your father, as he will

have left work, so you must stay here until he returns and tell him what's happened. I'll ring from the hospital as soon as I find out how he is."

Within minutes, she had grabbed her coat and was driving to the Casualty Department. Being familiar with the hospital and the receptionists, she was immediately shown to the cubicle where Danny was lying. The doctor was waiting outside to give her a report before she saw Danny.

"How is he?"

"It was a nasty fall, but he has come out of it better than expected. He has broken his right arm and has bruised his ribs, which will cause discomfort for a few days, but it could have been worse. We'll keep him in overnight for observation but he should be able to come home tomorrow."

"Thank you, doctor. Can I see him?"

"Of course."

He took Mrs Watson to where Danny was lying and she was pleased to see him quite cheerful, although she could see that he was in pain when he moved.

After she had telephoned Mr Watson and Karen, she remained for a short time making sure that Danny was as comfortable as possible. When she arrived home, she was pleased to find that Karen had been busy with the final preparations for the meal. It wasn't long before they were sitting at the table, but no one was really hungry. Instead of eating, Mrs Watson found herself answering questions about Danny's accident. Eventually the meal was finished and the family was able to make its way to the hospital. It was a large place with buildings spread over a wide area, so Karen was pleased her mother knew exactly which part to make for, even though by this time the hospital was busy.

When Karen arrived on the ward she gave a quiet chuckle when she saw Danny with his arm in plaster.

"Can I write on it?" she asked immediately.

"Not until I get home and then I might let you if you're kind to me. It will give you an opportunity to practise your nursing skills."

When the family returned home they all agreed that the house would seem quiet without Danny.

However, the following day he was allowed home and soon became used to using his left hand. Writing, though, was almost impossible for him.

On the following Sunday, Danny received much attention from his friends at church and to be honest, he quite enjoyed it.

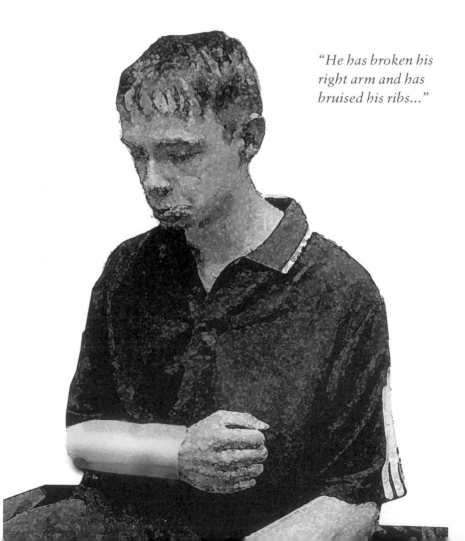

"He has broken his right arm and has bruised his ribs…"

When Rachel came in the afternoon, she was sympathetic to Danny and he was really pleased. His father then reminded them that it was time to look at the next statement in the Lord's Prayer.

"Can someone tell me the next verse?"

"Your Kingdom come, Your will…"

"Hold it Rachel!" interrupted Mr Watson. "I know you're keen, but we'll just look at the first part today."

He began to explain that only those who are Christians can pray this prayer. Those who oppose Christ and break His law cannot pray this prayer.

"In these words of Jesus we are told that God is a King because only Kings have Kingdoms. He has a royal title and holds signs of royalty. Can you tell me what a King wears?" asked Mr Watson.

"A crown," answered Karen—grateful for an easy question.

"And what does he carry?"

"A sceptre," replied Rachel.

"Anything else?"

"A sword," said Danny.

"That's good. Now God has all these signs of royalty, because He is a great King. He has not become great, He is great," emphasised Mr Watson with strong conviction. "Why is He great?"

"Because He has power over people and because He made everything," replied Karen.

"Don't forget He not only made everything, but can destroy everything," added her mother.

"He also knows everything," joined in Danny, "and sees everything."

"That means He is everywhere," added Rachel always determined not to be left out.

Mr Watson then went on to explain that no earthly King can be compared to God, because God is King of all kings, and His Kingdom will never end because He lives forever. As God is a great King, with a vast Kingdom, we are wise to serve and follow Him. It is important for us to be on the strongest side and, when we belong to Him, we are.

Mr Watson then encouraged the youngsters to trust God with their lives because they could not put them in safer hands. God can never fail and He can do what to us seems impossible. He will help us through our greatest problems.

"Can I interrupt a moment?" asked Mrs Watson. "Your father said God can do the impossible to protect his children. Can you think of any examples from the Bible?"

Danny immediately thought of the story in Exodus when God brought the children of Israel through the Red Sea and destroyed the Egyptian army.

"There is also the story of Daniel who was protected from the lions," added Rachel.

"And the three friends of Daniel who were thrown into the fiery furnace," remembered Karen.

> "...let us remember that as Christians, God's Kingdom is within us. As King, He rules every part of us and because of this, His presence is very real".

"You mean Shadrach, Meshach and Abednego," answered her father realising that she could not remember the names. "The important point to remember is that even if we lose our life and possessions, God will give us His peace and a home in heaven."

"What does the word 'Kingdom' mean?" asked Rachel with a puzzled expression, "or what Kingdom is Jesus talking about?"

"That's a good question," replied Mr Watson. "He certainly didn't mean a political Kingdom, because He told Pilate that His Kingdom was not in this world. Even the disciples thought His Kingdom belonged on this earth. What He really meant was a Kingdom of grace which would be in our hearts. Today people are in a Kingdom of darkness. They have no knowledge of God's love and they prefer to stay like that."

"Do you remember working on the garden last spring, Danny?" interrupted his mother. "When you and your father moved the concrete slabs which had piled up during the winter, the different insects ran in every direction to escape the light because they were happier in the darkness.

"Yes, I do"

"Well," continued his mother, "people are similar to those insects and prefer living lives that are bad and dark rather than living in goodness and the light of God's Kingdom."

"I suppose," said Karen, "that when we pray like this, we are asking God to end the Kingdom of the Devil."

"That's right," answered her father.

He then went on to explain that we are also praying that the Kingdom of Heaven will come quickly and that when the time comes, we will be taken to it. Before we can go to the Kingdom of Heaven, we must first have faith in Jesus Christ as our Saviour.

"It's like a seed that becomes a flower," remarked Mrs Watson. "It has to be a seed first. We must become a Christian before we can enter God's Kingdom in Heaven."

"Now before we finish," said Mr Watson, "let us remember that as Christians, God's Kingdom is within us. As King, He rules every part of us and because of this, His presence is very real. We can, as members of God's family, pray this prayer and until we arrive in Heaven, we must continue to pray it. When we do reach Heaven, we shall enjoy all that is good. No more sickness, no more pain, no more sorrow, no more death; and Danny - no more doubts."

"And no more broken arms!" added Danny, before Mr Watson closed with a prayer.

Danny gets bored

It was a week since Danny's accident and the special attention, which he had received during the first few days, was beginning to fade.

There was little he could do apart from play on his computer and he soon began to wish his left arm had been broken instead of his right. At least he could then write or draw. His mother was very much aware that Danny was bored and so tried to involve him with as many things as possible.

"Cheer up misery! You look as though you've lost five pounds and found ten pence," said Karen as she bounced through the door on return from school.

Danny was pleased to see Karen return. There were very few dull moments when his sister was around.

"Oh, I'm just fed up not being able to use this arm," he replied dejectedly.

"You were enjoying the attention a week ago," his mother reminded him as she entered the room.

"Not any longer!"

"Mum," said Karen suddenly, "can you spare a minute?"

"As long as it is a minute. I haven't begun to get the dinner ready yet."

"It's just that a girl in my class called Jerusha.... "

"Called what?" interrupted Danny, never having heard the name before.

"Jerusha. I like it very much," insisted Karen.

"It's different," replied Danny.

"Anyway, don't interrupt me, it's important. Jerusha has her birthday next week, but her father has just become unemployed. They are very worried about the future and I don't think they can afford to give Jerusha a party. I was wondering if we could arrange one and invite them here."

"I think that's a great idea," said Danny enthusiastically.

"What do you think Mum?" asked Karen with hesitation in her voice.

"We'll see what we can do. I'll have a word with your father when he returns home."

During the evening Mrs Watson kept her promise and spoke to her husband about Karen's suggestion. They both agreed that it would not only please Karen, but would help and be a witness to Jerusha's parents.

Karen was delighted with the news, as was Danny, and both promised to help with the preparations for the party to be held in a fortnight's time.

When Jerusha and her parents were told of Karen's invitation, they were very grateful that someone had thought about them.

The remainder of that week went by very quickly and it wasn't long before the family members were gathered for their weekly discussion.

"What are we discussing this Sunday?" asked Mr Watson, looking at Rachel.

"Your will be done, on earth as it is in Heaven," she replied with a slight grin.

"But what do we mean by doing the will of God?" he asked, looking for a reply to his question.

"Doesn't it mean that we should do all that He tells us?" asked Danny, a little unsure of his reply.

"I think it means obeying Him by doing what He says," said Karen with confidence.

"In the Bible we are told what God wants us to do and if we obey Him, we are doing His will."

"All of you are right," replied Mr Watson. "It is important that we know God's will and then do it. To know God's will and not do it is very serious indeed."

"Doesn't it say somewhere else that we have not only to hear but to do? I can't think where," asked Karen.

"Perhaps I can help," suggested Mrs Watson. "You're thinking of James. Our minister was preaching from that book only a few weeks ago."

"It shows some were listening," said Danny a little ashamed that he had forgotten.

The conversation continued upon this line for some time until Rachel, who had been quiet for a while, shared another thought.

"I've been thinking,"

"Congratulations!" interrupted Danny.

"To know and do God's will shows our love for Jesus. If we love Him, we will do what pleases Him, and if we don't, it must be sinful as well as silly."

"You're on good form today, Rachel," said Mr Watson, delighted at Rachel's progress.

"Could I also add one other point?" asked Mrs Watson. "Doing God's will on earth makes us more like Jesus and that must be our greatest desire."

"That's right," agreed her husband. "But let's go a step further. How do we do God's will?"

"By loving Jesus," answered Karen.

"Yes, but how do we show that we love Jesus?"

"That's easy," said Danny quickly. "We show that we love Him by putting Him first."

"That's easy to say, but more difficult to do," replied his father.

"I remember when we discussed the Commandments," said Rachel, "you told us to have no other gods before the only God. He must come before our hobbies, our possessions and our friends."

For more than half an hour they shared ways in which they could do God's will. Then Danny thought of his personal problem.

"Dad, is it God's will that my arm is broken?"

"Many things happen in life that are not pleasant. Christians lose loved ones; they become unemployed; they face poverty; they even become ill and suffer far longer than you will. God uses us in each situation; and has many things to teach us—including patience."

That hit Danny where it hurt, because he knew that he was becoming very impatient not being able to do what he enjoyed doing, particularly playing cricket.

"But how can we discover God's will?" asked Karen. "How can I know what God wants me to do? When I make decisions that affect my future, how can I be sure it is what God wants me to do and where He wants me to go..."

"Hold it!" said her father with a smile; "we can only answer one question at a time although your questions are very similar. Come on, who can answer Karen's questions?"

"By reading the Bible," replied Danny. "The more we know the Bible, the more we learn God's will for us."

"That's right," replied his father. "God has given each of us a brain and a Bible. If we use both, we can discover the plan God has for our lives. Any more contributions?"

"God can use our abilities," answered Rachel. "My parents bought me a computer recently and, in time, I could use my talent for God. This could be His will for me."

"Our minister is good at talking to young people," said Mrs Watson. "By using this gift, he is doing God's will."

They continued for the rest of the afternoon talking about the many ways God's will may be done and how we can know His will. These included using our gifts, and also accepting advice from mature Christians. On each occasion they returned to the importance of the Bible which must, after all, be the final word in knowing and doing God's will.

"Come on, Karen," said Mr Watson. "It's time for tea, both for us and for Lassie."

With a stretch and wag of her tail, Lassie followed Karen to where her dog biscuits and meat were kept. She had no intention of being late for tea and, with a lick of her lips, was determined to enjoy it.

Chapter 7

Party time for Jerusha

It was Monday morning and the twins were up early for a change. Danny was eager to be going back to school after a week at home, which had dragged by far too slowly. He was looking forward to the attention from his friends and wondered how many autographs he could get on his plaster cast. Dare he ask his teacher? Perhaps not.

"Now don't be late home," shouted Mrs Watson from the kitchen. "There's a lot of work to do for Jerusha's party. I hope you have asked her parents. Anyway, I'll give them a call this morning to remind them."

"Thanks," replied Karen.

"See you later," called Danny as they both made their way through the front door.

The day went by without any problems for the twins. Both had a good day at school and, to Mrs Watson's relief, were home in good time.

"Wow!" exclaimed Karen as she walked into the kitchen. "You have been busy. They look great."

"They really do," joined in Danny.

Mrs Watson had spent the whole day preparing for the party. On the table there was a chocolate cake decorated with smarties, a coffee cake, a sponge with cherries, a walnut cake and many assorted buns. Also on the table was a square box, which made the twins very curious.

"What's in that?" asked Danny.

"Would you like to look?" replied Mrs Watson, as she carefully lifted the lid.

"I didn't know you were getting a special cake," said Karen with surprise. "It looks lovely."

"You can't have a birthday without a cake. Do you like the words and colour of the icing?" their mother enquired.

"It looks brilliant," they replied together, not sure what words to use.

"Come on then, staring time is over. There is a lot more to be done, as these need to go in the freezer to keep them fresh for the party; it will save time later in the week."

When the evening meal was over, Karen got down to her homework and then turned her attention to helping her mother in the preparations. Danny spent the evening planning how to decorate the lounge and organise the games.

The day of the party soon arrived, and Mrs Watson was relieved that everything was ready for the great invasion.

On the stroke of five o'clock, friends of Jerusha and Karen began to arrive. Unfortunately Danny was the only boy, but that didn't stop him from enjoying himself.

The youngsters soon tucked into the tea, after Mr Watson had thanked God for the food. Within half an hour, a good demolition job had been done!

Jerusha's parents joined in all the games, as did Mr and Mrs Watson. By ten o'clock everyone was worn out. It had been a great success and Jerusha and her parents were very grateful for all that had been done for them.

There was another member of the family who had enjoyed herself. That was Lassie. She had loved the attention given to her and had romped around all evening. It wasn't long before she was in her basket fast asleep.

The remainder of the week soon passed by. When Sunday came, the weather was dull and much cooler. The trees had now shed most of their leaves and everything in the garden was looking lifeless. Inside, the fire was glowing brightly and it felt warm and cosy.

Rachel arrived at the usual time, buried in her brightly coloured coat.

"A cup of coffee?" asked Mrs Watson, as Rachel made her way into the lounge and sat as near to the fire as Lassie would let her.

Very soon they were all ready to talk about the next phrase in the Lord's Prayer - 'Give us this day our daily bread'.

"We come to an important change in this prayer," said Mr Watson as he introduced the subject. "Can anyone think what it is?"

They all looked puzzled and remained silent.

"Let me tell you then. The first three statements concern God's glory. Now we come to our personal concerns. You see, God's glory must come before our needs."

"I can see that now," said Danny. "Why couldn't I see it before?"

"I didn't see it until someone pointed it out," replied Mrs Watson. "We never get past the age of learning. The important thing is that we do learn and remember."

"We have thought about God's glory during the past three weeks," continued Mr Watson. "Now we come to our needs - not our wants."

"What do you mean?" asked Rachel.

"Can I answer that?" asked Karen confidently.

Mr Watson gave a gentle nod of his head and Karen continued.

"There are a lot of things we want, but very few things we need."

"I couldn't have put it better myself," he replied, "I'll remember that, when your next request comes."

Karen looked at her father with a little grin, wishing she had not been so quick with the answer.

"What we need to remember," said Mrs Watson, changing the subject to save Karen's blushes, "is that God gives us many things such as our home, our car, our food as well as our life. God can take them away as easily as He gives them. You would have no food if the sun didn't shine or the rain fall."

"In my Quiet Time," said Rachel, "I'm reading the book of Exodus, and I remember how the Israelites had no food or water but God met their needs in giving them both. Without God's help they would have died."

"That's a good example," agreed Mr Watson. "The other thing to remember is that they didn't deserve God's help, and neither do we."

"A thought has just come to me," interrupted Mrs Watson. "Everything we have is a gift from God - such as wisdom, peace, our health, the sun and the rain. We cannot exist without Him."

"Why don't people thank God for these things?" asked Danny.

"Because we are selfish and our hearts are sinful," replied Karen thoughtfully.

"That was a very good question and an equally good reply," said Mr Watson. "It reminds me of an amusing story I heard some time ago. It was about a farmer from Devon who came to London for an agricultural exhibition. He arrived in the city during the morning and went to a cafe for a meal. Being a Christian, he offered God a prayer of thanks for his food and as he was saying grace, a group of young lads started to laugh. When he had finished praying, he asked the lads, "do you ever give thanks to God for your food". They laughed and replied, "of course we don't".

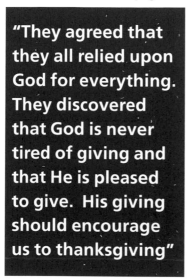

"They agreed that they all relied upon God for everything. They discovered that God is never tired of giving and that He is pleased to give. His giving should encourage us to thanksgiving"

"Funny, that", the farmer replied, "neither do my pigs"

The lads stopped laughing and clearly understood the message."

"I think we do as well," answered Rachel with some amusement at the story.

As they continued talking, they agreed that they all relied upon God for everything. They discovered that God is never tired of giving and that He is pleased to give. Mr Watson also pointed out that God is different to us because He gives to His enemies, even though they don't thank Him. His giving should encourage us to thanksgiving. Mr Watson was ready to close the discussion, but as he was going to pray Danny asked a question, which needed an answer.

"It says 'give us this day.' Does that mean it is wrong to save for the future?"

"The Bible says that we are responsible in providing for our families," replied Mrs Watson. "But Jesus taught us this prayer so that we should not worry about the future, for He will provide for us day by day."

"Time has gone by," said Mr Watson. "We must look at Danny's question in more detail on another occasion, because he has raised an important subject."

The family just had time for a quick snack before they went to church. Although they were in a hurry, they still made time to thank God for their daily bread.

Problems at the office

It was just after five o'clock and the telephone rang as Mrs Watson was preparing the vegetables for the evening meal. She ran to the 'phone, drying her hands on the way.

"Hello."

"It's me dear," answered her husband. "I'm going to be very late for dinner. You have yours with the children, and you can put mine in the microwave when I get back."

"You sound very annoyed. What's gone wrong?"

"I can't tell you on the telephone, but I'll explain when I get back. I hope it won't be too late, but don't worry, it's nothing too serious."

It was half past eight when the door opened and Mr Watson entered the house. He put his briefcase down beside the bookcase and collapsed into the chair with a sigh.

"It sounds as though things haven't gone too well," said his wife as she sat on the settee near his chair. Even Lassie tried to show some sympathy as she put her head on his knee.

"It's a long story, but Simon, one of the office staff, carelessly lost some important information on the computer and it has taken nearly six hours to correct the fault. It was such a stupid thing to do."

"Has he apologised?" his wife asked.

"Oh yes, he was very sorry, but sometimes it's so difficult to forgive, especially when it seemed so unnecessary."

"But we must," she replied. "Perhaps it may be our mistake next time and we will need someone to forgive us."

"Yes, I know you are right, but... I think I'll feel better after a good meal."

"Hint accepted," said his wife as she made her way to the kitchen.

Mrs Watson, although a busy person, always had time to listen to her family's problems. Tonight her husband appreciated her calm and thoughtful words. When she returned with his meal, he remembered to thank her.

The following morning Mr Watson set off for work determined to put the events of the previous day behind him. He was going to see Simon immediately and assure him that his apology, which was genuine, had been accepted.

As the weekend approached, the weather became much colder and Mrs Watson noticed that it was nearly dark by the time the children returned from school. The twins had heard their father tell stories of going to school in snow- drifts well before Christmas when he lived in Yorkshire. Wouldn't it be great if this cold weather brought snow, as the following day was the first Sunday in December.

When they woke up the next morning there was no snow to be seen, but the clouds were heavy and the forecast had said that snow was a possibility.

When the family returned from the morning service, Karen and her mother soon had the dinner prepared and everyone had a very healthy appetite.

"Come on, Karen, your turn to wash the dishes," said her father.

"When I get married the first thing I buy will be a dishwasher," she replied.

"And remember, young man," said his father turning to Danny with a grin, "when you have that plaster off, you'll be washing dishes right up to Christmas."

"And beyond," added Karen.

It wasn't long before they were drinking coffee in the lounge ready to turn to the next verse in the Lord's Prayer. Rachel arrived and soon made herself at home with the family.

"Now, where are we?" asked Mr Watson.

"Forgive us our debts as we forgive our debtors," replied Rachel without hesitation.

"Yes, I should have remembered that after the events of last week," said Mr Watson, glancing across the room at his wife. They both smiled at each other.

"Last week," he continued, "we looked at a part of the Lord's Prayer that concerned the body. Today and next Sunday we look at two phrases which refer to our souls. Which are the most important?"

"Our souls," replied Karen.

"Why do you say that?" asked her father.

"Because our bodies will die but our souls will live forever."

> **"On the cross, Jesus took our place. He died instead of us so that our sins would be forgiven. Our debt was paid. Only He can forgive us."**

"Can I join in here?" asked Mrs Watson. "In our schools, why do we give hours of education for our bodies and minds, yet so little, if any, to our souls which will live beyond death?"

"Good question," replied her husband. "It just shows how, in our country, we have our priorities completely wrong."

"I suppose we can get it wrong even as Christians," suggested Danny.

"What do you mean?" asked Karen.

"Well, we spend a lot of money and time looking after our body, but forget our souls."

"You're right," said his father. "Now let's come to the words of this prayer. Our 'debts' is another word for sin, so for the moment you can forget about any money you owe me. Luke, in fact, uses the word 'sin' in his Gospel, Chapter 11 and verse 4.

"Why is sin called a debt?" asked Rachel.

"If someone owes me money and refuses to give it," replied Mr Watson, "they are not paying what should be mine. They are in my debt. A person who is in debt is guilty of not paying and can go to prison."

"We owe God a lot," said Karen thoughtfully. "We should give to Him our love and obedience, and if we don't, I suppose we are in debt to Him, and need His forgiveness."

"That's right," agreed her mother. "We owe God a great deal, but we have nothing to pay Him for what we owe. We are in His debt."

"Isn't it good that God forgets our debts when we ask Him to forgive us," said Danny thankfully.

"We must always remember that our debts are against our Creator and that they are many. Notice that it says debts and not debt," Mr Watson continued. "No other person can pay the debts for us."

"Jesus can!" said Rachel confidently.

"You got there first," Mr Watson answered. "On the cross, Jesus took our place. He died instead of us so that our sins would be forgiven. Our debt was paid. Only He can forgive us."

They talked for quite a while on God's forgiveness. Mr Watson used the illustration of a cork which rises to the surface if thrown into water. He told them that God's forgiveness was not like a cork, but like lead which will sink to the bottom, never to be seen again. All our sins are buried out of our sight, cast into the depths of the sea and never to be remembered anymore.

"Look at the time!" interrupted Mrs Watson. "It's nearly four o'clock, and we have still to look at the other part of forgiveness."

"We can leave that until next week," suggested her husband.

"No" replied Karen immediately, "we can all help with the tea."

"I'll hold you to that," laughed her mother.

Mr Watson continued without a further word from anyone.

"Now we have looked at the words, 'forgive us our debts', but then it says 'as we forgive our debtors'. In other words we are to forgive those who sin against us. How do we do that?"

"I thought only God could forgive sin?" asked Rachel, a little puzzled.

"If we sin against God, only He can forgive us," replied Mr Watson. "But if another person sins against us, we may forgive them."

"I find it very hard to forgive when someone has hurt and been nasty to me," said Rachel honestly.

"We all do," admitted Mrs Watson. "When we are angry and do not forgive, it shows weakness. When we do forgive it shows strength. A person may be unkind to us, but if we do not forgive them when they have said they are sorry, we are even more unkind."

"Why should we always forgive people?" asked Danny.

"Well, you have asked the question, now see if you can answer it," suggested his father.

"Can I answer?" asked Karen. "We should forgive because Jesus did. On the cross He asked God to forgive those who crucified Him."

"Well done! That means we should be like Jesus. He forgives us, so we should forgive others - and remember, God forgives us often." Mr Watson continued with a warning. "If we do not forgive others, then we cannot expect God to forgive us."

"I don't like to stop this conversation," said Mrs Watson, "but we must get something ready to eat quickly before we go to church."

"Let's have a prayer before we close," suggested her husband. "We can ask God to forgive our sins and help us to forgive those who have sinned against us."

The snow begins to fall

All that week the clouds had been dark and heavy. On Saturday afternoon, the twins were busy completing their homework and although Mr Watson had a book in his hands, his eyes were beginning to close. Mrs Watson had just finished the ironing and curled up on the settee with her magazine and a tempting box of chocolates.

"It's snowing!" shouted Karen as she jumped on a chair near the window.

"Hey! Chairs are for sitting on," called out her mother with a firm voice.

Karen immediately jumped off the chair, but was quickly joined by Danny and for the next few minutes they watched excitedly as the first snowflakes began to fall. Mr Watson had unfortunately been disturbed from his afternoon sleep. His book had fallen on Lassie who remained in exactly the same position. She was too comfortable to even think of moving.

It was unusual to see snow so early in December, especially in the south of England. In fact, there hadn't been any snow at all for the past few years.

"I think it's getting heavier," said Danny excitedly.

"Do you think it will keep snowing?" asked Karen hopefully.

"We'll have to wait and see," replied Mr Watson, still half-asleep.

It continued to snow all afternoon until it became so dark that it was difficult to see. From time to time the twins would look through the window at the streetlights and they could see the snow falling quite heavily.

A few hours later they went to bed very excited, hoping that in the morning the roads and paths would be covered with snow.

When they got up the next day, they were not disappointed. The snow was a few inches deep, and even better, it was still falling.

"Hurry up, you two," shouted Mr Watson. "After breakfast, I need some help clearing the snow from the garage doors. It's my turn to collect some of the older people for church today."

Soon they were downstairs eating their breakfast and then out shovelling the snow. This was great fun although, as they moved it, it began to settle again very quickly. As they were busy working, the twins were hoping that the snow would still be there the following Saturday. If so they would go down to Lodge Hill which was perfect for sledging.

The morning service had been well attended despite the weather, but the congregation looked almost like a group of walking snowmen. With a strong north wind blowing, some of them felt like snowmen!

"Put the kettle on please, Karen," said Mr Watson when they arrived home. "Dinner won't be long," assured Mrs Watson, as the battle with the wind had given everyone a healthy appetite.

"That's the best dinner I've had since yesterday," said Karen as she leaned back in her chair. "I'm sure I've eaten too much."

"I've just the answer to your problem," said her father. "Gentle action such as washing up will make you feel more comfortable."

Sometimes it's better to say nothing, thought Karen as she slowly made her way to the kitchen sink.

The job was soon done and they were settling into their seats with all eyes directed upon Mr Watson.

"We are gradually coming to the final part of the Lord's Prayer. Who can tell me the next verse?"

"Lead us not into temptation," replied Rachel as she rushed into the room and sat as near to the fire as possible. "But I thought that was something God wouldn't do."

"Hey! You are quick this afternoon," said Mr Watson. "You've raised an important point, for God does not tempt anyone[2]. He lets people sin, but will never encourage it; instead He tells people to live holy lives. After all, no ruler would tempt people to break the laws which he himself has made."

"Last month I began reading the book of Genesis[3] and it says that God tested Abraham. How do we explain this?" asked Mrs Watson.

"Good question," replied her husband.

Karen immediately turned her eyes to her father and wondered how he would answer this one.

"When I left school ..."

"Last century," interrupted Danny, which brought a smile to his father's face.

"May I continue? ... I worked in a jewellery shop and on one occasion we had a lesson on the refining of gold. It has to be heated many times until the metal is pure and the goldsmith can see his reflection in it. We go through times of trial and testing until we become the people God wants us to be, and His Son is seen in our lives. There is a big difference between being tempted and tested. God tempts nobody, but He did test Abraham and from time to time He will test us. However, it will make us better people."

"What does 'lead us not into temptation' really mean then?" asked Karen, still looking at her father.

"I think it means that we ask God, who loves us very much, not to let us be tempted so that we fall into sin."

"If God doesn't tempt us so that we sin, who does?" asked Rachel.

"You're asking me many questions today. How about someone else answering this one," suggested Mr Watson.

"If God does not tempt us, then the Devil is responsible," said Danny with confidence. "I believe he was called the 'the tempter' when Jesus met him in the wilderness."

"I thought Jesus defeated the Devil when He died for us," said Karen.

"He did," replied Mrs Watson. "He is like a prisoner who has been sentenced, waiting for the punishment to be carried out. Until then he will cause as much trouble in the world as he possibly can. We may face him anywhere, and he will find us even when we are reading and praying. In this life we will always face temptation, but as Jesus won the victory over the Devil, so must we."

"It's like the hymn we sing sometimes," suggested Rachel. "Yield not to temptation, for yielding is sin. Each victory will help us some other to win."

"I'm pleased Rachel has caused us to consider the Devil," said Mr Watson. "We must never forget the danger we can be in from temptations."

They began to consider the Christian's enemy, realising that the Devil will do anything within his power to destroy our happiness. He does not waste time, he is always busy, and he has more than one way of tempting us. If one plan fails, he will always find another.

They also discussed the power of the Devil and found that he is called 'the strong man'. He has power to reach our hearts, thoughts and wills. He also knows the best time to tempt us.

"We may have to continue with this part of the Lord's Prayer next week as our time has nearly gone," said Mr Watson, realising that they hadn't even started to consider the second part of the phrase.

The afternoon had been so helpful that the youngsters had not realised that the snow had stopped falling.

"There is one point I wish to mention to you youngsters," continued Mr Watson. "When we are converted to Christ, our faith is weak, and temptations appear strong. The devil hates young Christians and will do all he can to bring them back to himself."

"He won't have me back," said Karen firmly.

"We pray daily that he won't have any of you," replied Mrs Watson with a note of concern. "Do be on your guard though, because there are so many temptations that you will have to face. Remember you will always have our support and don't be afraid of coming to us if you are in trouble."

"That goes for me too," said her husband. "Next week we'll look at some other ways by which the Devil leads us into temptation, and hopefully we will have time to look at the remainder of the verse."

Danny has his plaster removed

Danny's arm had healed quicker than everyone expected and today he would be going back to the hospital hoping that the plaster would be taken off.

"Will it hurt?" he asked his mother.

"Not really. You see, you are a Jacob."

"What do you mean? I thought I was Danny."

"In Genesis, Jacob had fair skin with not much hair on his arms. His brother Esau had quite a lot of hair. If a plaster is on hairy arms, it can hurt a bit when it is taken off, but you should have no problem."

When Danny and his mother arrived at the hospital, it wasn't long before they saw the doctor and soon the plaster was removed. Danny's arm felt much lighter but, at first, he was scared to use it.

When he arrived home he couldn't wait to show Karen and his father what the doctor had done. He hadn't waited long before Karen returned from school.

"Hey, that looks much better," said Karen when she noticed the plaster had been removed. "No excuses now when you are asked to do something, or will you find some new ones?"

"Now don't be nasty."

"Sorry. I really am pleased.... honestly."

Mr Watson returned from work two hours later. He had been very busy at the office and was looking forward to a quiet evening at home.

"Oh! What do I see here?" he asked, looking at Danny. "I guess you're glad to have that plaster off. How does it feel?"

"Fine," replied Danny. "Dad, could I go sledging on Saturday? Some of my friends at school are going to Lodge Hill."

"What do you think?" he asked, turning to his wife.

"I think he'll be OK if he's careful. We can't keep him in cotton wool."

"Great! Thanks Mum."

What an exciting afternoon they had. Lodge Hill was perfect for sledging and the weather was dry with a clear sky. How they wished every winter brought this amount of snow. It wasn't just the youngsters who took the opportunity to enjoy the conditions - many adults were there too.

"Enjoy yourself?" asked his mother as he returned home.

"It was great. You should have come."

"No thanks! I'm getting too old for that. We had our opportunity when we lived up north. By the way, tea will be ready soon, so hurry up and get yourself out of those wet clothes."

"I'm starving. Won't be long," Danny replied as he raced upstairs two steps at a time.

During the night the weather changed. The temperature had fallen and icicles began to hang from the gutters. It seemed that the sledging could continue for a while at least. The Watsons certainly found it more difficult getting to church than they had the previous Sunday, as did most people in the congregation.

"Come on," said Mr Watson when dinner had ended. "We must not be too late starting."

"Rachel hasn't arrived yet," replied Karen.

"I think she has," said her mother hearing the doorbell ring.

Rachel left her boots in the porch and made her way to the lounge. She would not miss these afternoons for anything.

"Now, where were we?" asked Mr Watson as he opened his Bible. "We must try and finish verse thirteen today. Can anyone remember the points we discussed last week?"

"I can," said Karen at once.

"OK! It's over to you," said Mr Watson as he settled back in his chair. During the next few minutes Karen covered nearly every area of the conversation leaving little more to be said.

"Well done!" said Mrs Watson, always ready to encourage.

"Who's a clever girl then?" exclaimed Danny, surprised that his sister had remembered so much.

Karen did not reply, but it was clear that she was pleased with herself, although a little embarrassed.

"Let's look at some other times when the Devil tempts us," suggested Mr Watson. "What about people who are unemployed?"

"I sometimes find it difficult during the long holidays," said Danny. "When you don't know what to do, the Devil can lead you in the wrong direction. He even gets you to think of wrong things. That's why I plan my holidays carefully."

"That's very sensible," replied his father.

"But what about people who are retired?" asked Rachel. "I think it's very important for people to be involved in church or charity work."

"These are all good suggestions," said Mrs Watson. "We must be busy and active because the devil finds wrong tasks for idle people. Are there any other times when we feel tempted?"

"I often feel the Devil attacks after a service or prayer meeting," admitted Mrs Watson. "You would think this is the worst time for him to tempt us. Perhaps it's because we relax and feel too secure. I suppose it can be compared to someone who has had a good meal and then feels sleepy. I have heard people say that following the mountain-top experience we can soon find ourselves in the valley."

Our minister has said something similar," added Mr Watson. "When he's been aware of God's help in preaching, he often feels aware of the Devil's attack. The story of the Lord's baptism is a good example.4 Following that wonderful experience, He was soon aware of the Devil's temptations in the wilderness."5

"It seems that he is around at all times," said Karen thoughtfully. "I suppose we must be ready for an attack at any time and in any place."

"I couldn't have summed it up better," replied Mr Watson. "But don't you think the Devil also tempts us when we are at our weakest?"

"I find him near me when I am alone," suggested Karen. "When we are together like this I feel strong enough for anything."

"You are not the only one," admitted Danny. "I suppose the Garden of Eden is a good example. The Devil attacked Eve when she was by herself. If she had kept close to Adam, she might not have taken the fruit."

"If she had kept close to God, it would have been even better," said Mrs Watson. "I suppose that is a lesson for all of us."

> "We must do all we can to make sure that we do not fall into temptation. First we must avoid being alone when the devil attacks. In Ecclesiastes it says 'Two are better than one'. To be in the company of other Christians is a good remedy against the enemy."

They continued to discuss other occasions when they had felt the Devil's temptations. Being a nurse, Mrs Watson had known people who had been tempted during times of illness and when loved ones had suddenly died in sad circumstances.

Mr Watson reminded them that they must be aware that the Devil tempts people to sin gradually. We might even be unaware that we are being tempted.

As he was speaking, Mr Watson glanced at the clock and was surprised to see how quickly the afternoon had passed by.

"Let's remind ourselves of the lessons we have learned," he said, "We must do all we can to make sure that we do not fall into temptation. First we must avoid being alone when the devil attacks. In Ecclesiastes it says 'Two are better than one'. To be in the company of other Christians is a good remedy against the enemy."

"I hope that when we have finished the Lord's Prayer we can look at something else," said Rachel. "It has helped me very much."

"I can't see why not," replied Mrs Watson.

"Secondly," continued Mr Watson, "never be idle. When a person has nothing to do, problems come. Thirdly, share your problem with a friend whom you trust. Finally, find time to pray and read God's Word; it is the sword of the Spirit."

"I thought we were going to look at the second part of this verse," said Karen, eager to continue.

"So did I," replied her father. "We must do so next week or else we won't have finished before the Christmas holidays.

"What are you doing at Christmas?" Karen asked Rachel.

"Just a minute, you two," interrupted Mrs Watson. "There are more immediate matters to deal with, such as getting something to eat."

"Hear! Hear!" said Danny, patting his stomach.

Flood warning

During the early part of that week, there was no change in the weather. Although the main roads were now clear of snow, the side streets were still covered and driving was very difficult. The youngsters loved it, but older people found walking dangerous.

It was Wednesday evening and Mr Watson was listening to the news and weather forecast while his wife was finishing baking in the kitchen.

"It seems a change is on the way," he shouted out to his wife.

"What do you mean?" she asked, walking into the room drying her hands.

"They are predicting a sudden rise in temperature which might lead to some flooding. Don't forget we have the river at the bottom of the garden and the level of water is high already."

"Yes, but we do have a wall to protect us," she replied, "and it would have to be bad to reach the house."

"I was really thinking of the row of bungalows which only have short gardens and older people living in them."

The following day, the weather did change. By the afternoon a number of roads were flooding and the river was in danger of bursting its banks. The Fire Brigades were busy pumping out drains that could not take any more water.

The local Council was busy stacking sacks of sand against the doors of homes near the river. The local radio and television were broadcasting warnings and advising people not to travel unless it was absolutely necessary.

"I'm soaked!" said Danny as he returned from school.

"Go straight upstairs and get out of those wet clothes," his mother instructed without a second thought.

"Can I have a shower?" he asked.

"Wasn't the one you've been in good enough?" she replied with a smile.

It was not long before Karen returned in the same condition, and pleaded with her brother to hurry out of the shower.

"You look more like humans now," said their mother as the twins came downstairs.

"I'm hungry! How long will dinner be?" asked Danny, unconcerned as to what he may have looked like.

"It won't be too long. I think your father has just arrived home."

Mr Watson was wise enough to take a large golf umbrella after he heard the weather forecast, but he too was pleased to be home where it was warm and dry.

The following morning, the family woke up to see a clear sky which continued until the weekend.

To the relief of all - apart from the ducks - the ground was drying and the river was gradually falling towards a safe level.

The Lord's Day was a beautiful day, so different from the previous one when everyone found it difficult to reach the church. Today there wasn't a snowflake to be seen anywhere.

As soon as Rachel arrived at the Watson's house, the youngsters began to talk about their experiences earlier in the week.

"Hey, you three!" shouted Mr Watson above the noise of their conversation. "It sounds like Question Time in Parliament. Let's go to the front room and return to our discussion. I didn't expect to spend three Sundays on verse thirteen, so we must conclude this afternoon."

When they had settled down, Mr Watson asked Rachel to read the verse and tell them what she thought it meant.

"Deliver us from evil. I think it means that we are asking God to keep us from doing wrong and help us to do what is good."

"I think that is a good beginning. Can anybody else add to that?" asked Mr Watson.

"I'll try to," said Danny, "or we might be finishing in five minutes."

"Cheeky! Come on then, let's hear the expert," said his father with a slight grin.

"Rachel's right, but I'm not sure 'doing wrong' are the correct words."

"I see disagreement coming for the first time," said Karen. "This could be exciting."

"Let's see what Danny has to say," said her mother.

"...if we carry on sinning, we become under the control of the Devil even more. Those who serve the Devil have a bad master."

Danny began in the best way he could, to say that he did many things wrong, but he would not say that they were evil. He suggested that we are asking God to deliver us from sin.

"I agree with Danny," said Rachel.

"Oh! I didn't expect agreement to come so soon," responded Karen.

Mr Watson then began to explain that we are asking God to first of all deliver us from the evil in our own heart; then to deliver us from the evil in the world. All evil comes from the Devil, and we need to be kept from him. When we ask God to 'deliver us from evil' we are asking Him to deliver us from the evil of sin. Mr Watson then compared sin with a disease such as leprosy. It begins in a small way, but if untreated and uncontrolled it can have tragic results.

"I suppose," said Rachel listening very carefully, "that as leprosy can destroy a body, sin can destroy a soul."

"You have put that well," said Mrs Watson, always encouraged by Rachel's contribution and her keen interest.

"But what really is sin?" asked Karen thoughtfully. "I mean, we talk about it and say how bad it is, but we need to know exactly what it is."

"You're right," replied Danny firmly. He then looked at his father, wishing he hadn't spoken in case he was asked to answer Karen's question.

"OK, let's try and discover what sin is," suggested Mr Watson. "When we discussed the Ten Commandments, we saw that sin was the breaking of God's Law. It is living in a way which is completely opposite to God's wishes. Instead of pleasing God, we please ourselves."

"Can I have a say?" asked Mrs Watson, continuing without waiting for an answer. "Sin is also failing to thank God for all that He has done for us. We looked at this a few weeks ago. There are many who fail to remember that God feeds us, shelters us and clothes us. He gives us everything, including our breath. It is sad that people do not thank Him and this is sin."

"That's a good start. Any more ideas?" asked Mr Watson, looking at the youngsters who were deep in thought.

After a short pause, Rachel suggested that sin was dangerous, because it robbed a person of eternal life. Danny then commented that if we carry on sinning, we become under the control of the Devil even more. Those who serve the Devil have a bad master. After another pause, Karen, who was not going to be left out, suggested that people in other countries can go hungry as the result of greed and war, and this too is sin.

As no further comments were offered, Mr Watson suggested that sin could cause people to be very unhappy. He also said that the greatest privilege in life was to have peace with God. This can only come through knowing Jesus Christ as our Saviour.

They continued for a little longer, but again time was their greatest enemy. Although Danny enjoyed the discussions, he also looked forward to his tea.

"Next week we come to our last statement," said Mr Watson. "As the part-timers will begin their holidays before me, they should have plenty of time to think about it."

Christmas holidays begin

"Hi, Mum!" said Danny cheerfully as he returned home from school. "You seem full of beans," replied his mother as she began to feed Lassie, who was more concerned about the food in her bowl than noticing Danny in the hall.

"No more school for two weeks, " said Danny as he threw his case by the settee.

"Hey! I hope that is not staying there for a fortnight."

"I'll take it to my room in a minute."

It wasn't long before Mr Watson arrived home.

"You are very early tonight," his wife said as he walked through the front door.

"Yes, it's been quieter than most days, so we took the opportunity of leaving a little earlier to avoid the heavy traffic. It helps to make up for the times when I've had to work late."

"I'll start preparing dinner. Does roast beef and Yorkshire pudding interest you?" she asked.

The look on her husband's face told his wife she had made a good choice.

"Any post today?" asked Mr Watson as Danny ran downstairs.

"Only a holiday brochure," she replied.

"Can't we have Christmas before we think of summer holidays?" asked her husband.

"Dad, I've been thinking," said Danny as he settled in a chair near his father. "I noticed the holiday brochure and after talking to Karen, we wondered if next year we could have a different kind of holiday."

"You mean a holiday where you pay and not us.?"

"That wasn't what I had in mind," said Danny with a smile. "I wondered if we could have a holiday on a canal boat. A friend of mine at school had one last year, and he said it was brilliant. Karen's all in favour of it."

"I guess she is. We'll think about it, but not until the New Year."

"That's great."

"I only said 'think about it'. No promises have been made."

The week went by very quickly, with every member of the family preparing for the visitors who would be coming during Christmas and the New Year. When the Lord's Day came, everyone was ready for a welcome rest.

Following the morning church service, the Watsons returned home for dinner, bringing Rachel who had been invited to join them.

During the meal the conversation had centred on the service and how much they had enjoyed the afternoon discussions. When the meal was over, everyone helped with the dishes and then began to make their way into the front room.

"Well," began Mr Watson, "we have eventually come to the end of the Lord's Prayer and we must note how it tells us to give God all the praise. We began by looking to God, and we finish by again turning to Him. The first words remind us that His is the Kingdom. What do we mean by these words?"

"It means that He rules over everything," replied Karen. "He does have power and controls what He has created."

"That is true, but it also means that God will have the last word, because He is King," said Rachel.

"Very good. Next we read that He is the power. What does this say to us?" asked Mr Watson.

"It tells me that God can do anything," said Karen.

"He has done a lot already," said Rachel with enthusiasm. "He has created the world. That was a powerful thing to do, because what God has made looks so beautiful."

"Yes, but the death and resurrection of Jesus was even more beautiful and that also showed God's power," added Mrs Watson. "That is why every Lord's Day we remember it and therefore that day has become very important."

"It's encouraging," said Mr Watson, "to know that our God can do more than we can ever ask or think. There is no end to His power. There is more power hidden than all God has so far shown us. Now, what about His glory?"

For a moment there was silence. Then Mrs Watson asked a question. "What does the first Catechism say? You have been going through them at church."

"Man's chief end is to glorify God and to enjoy Him for ever," replied Karen. "Easy isn't it! Well, when you help us."

> "When we meet for worship in the church, we must make sure that in all we do, God is glorified. In our praying, singing and thinking, He must be lifted up as high as possible."

"That means that only God should have our praise." said Danny.

"Yes," replied Mr Watson. "When we meet for worship in the church, we must make sure that in all we do, God is glorified. In our praying, singing and thinking, He must be lifted up as high as possible."

"Well, we have now looked at the Ten Commandments and the Lord's Prayer," said Mrs Watson, before Danny suddenly interrupted her.

"We haven't finished yet," said Danny. "Don't forget the 'Amen'."

"You are right, Danny," said his father pleased that an important word had not been forgotten. "The word 'Amen' is a sign that we approve of what has been said. We are showing that we agree. That is why the congregation should say 'Amen' with the one who is praying, to show our agreement to what has been prayed. I think it is the last verse of Psalm 106 that says "Let all the people say, Amen."

After they had closed with prayer, Rachel had a confession to make.

"I always thought this day was boring, but it's been great to have been together and we have learned such a lot. I hope we can do something else next year."

"Any suggestions?" asked Mr Watson.

"What about the Sermon on the Mount?" suggested Mrs Watson.

"But that would take all next year," said Danny.

"Well, we could start with the Beatitudes," said his father, "perhaps we could study it when you have your summer holidays."

References

1,I John 4:8
2,I Corinthians 10:13
3,Genesis 22:1
4,Matthew 3
5,Matthew 4

Contents

Planning for a holiday

It was now the beginning of July, and both Karen and Danny were looking forward to a summer break from their studies. The past few months had not been easy as they had been preparing for their important exams which, fortunately, were now over. The difficult part was waiting for the results which would be known in a few weeks.

"Great! Just one week to go," said Danny as he threw his case and files on the settee and sat down beside them. "I hope we have better weather for the holiday."

"I'm sure it will improve," replied his mother as she began to set the table for dinner.

"What's for dinner, Mum?"

"I thought we would have a pizza."

"Did I hear pizza?" asked Karen as she returned from school. "The thought of my favourite meal makes a bad day good."

"It will be at least another half-hour before it is ready so you can take Lassie for a walk, she's in the garden."

An hour later the family were gathered around the table tucking into their evening meal and chatting quite freely about the events of the day. Mr Watson would ask Karen and Danny what they had done at school, then he and his wife would talk of how they had spent the day. It was the only meal when they were able to meet as a family and they valued the time to talk together.

During a brief pause in the conversation, Mr Watson brought up the subject of holidays and immediately every ear was attentive.

"You may remember that last December we discussed the possibility of having a canal boat holiday? Well, early this year I managed to book a canal boat for two weeks in August."

"That's brilliant!" cried the teenagers together.

"Where are we going?" asked Danny.

"I'm hoping to take you into the West Midlands, as I've been told there are a number of canals which go through some beautiful countryside."

"How long is the boat?" asked his wife.

"It will be about 75 foot long with at least four bedrooms."

"So that means we could take Rachel, couldn't we?" asked Karen with a hesitating finish to her question.

Mr Watson looked at his wife and Danny. Both nodded with approval.

"Can I ring her now?" asked Karen.

Fifteen minutes later Karen returned with a smile across her face, which revealed Rachel's response to the invitation.

"Well, we're waiting," said her father questioningly.

"Rachel thought the idea was great. She asked her parents and they are very pleased to get rid of her... I mean let her come with us. She also made a suggestion that while we are away, we could consider the Beatitudes. We did mention it after we finished the Ten Commandments and the Lord's Prayer."

"I am very pleased Rachel suggested this," replied her father. "I was thinking of beginning soon and continuing during the holidays. Anyway, I think your mother has more urgent matters on her mind such as washing up. When everything has been cleared away, you can invite Rachel round because I have some brochures to show you."

In record time the dishes were cleared, and the family began to make themselves comfortable waiting for Rachel's arrival.

When Rachel arrived she settled on the floor and Lassie came and snuggled by her.

"Can we take the dog?" she asked.

"I can't see why not," replied Mrs Watson, "After all, she is an important member of the family."

With that assurance Lassie gave a big yawn and fell asleep.

"Let's sit round the table, then we can see the brochures better," suggested Mrs Watson. "I'm afraid you will have to leave Lassie, Rachel."

After carefully moving Lassie's head from her lap she joined the others at the table.

"This is my plan," said Mr Watson as he opened the brochures at the right page. "I suggest we begin at Evesham and aim for the Avon Rings. We can call at places such as Stratford upon Avon…"

"Oh, I've done enough Shakespeare especially this year," interrupted Karen.

"You'll enjoy it," replied her father. "We can visit Warwick Castle, and many other sites. We will also cruise along the famous Grand Union Canal."

"Are there many canals?" asked Rachel already getting excited about the holiday.

"Yes, they cover most of the country. In fact there are over 1500 miles of waterway, including Scotland and Wales. There are some exciting journeys along the canals of Yorkshire."

"I wondered how long we would wait until Yorkshire was mentioned," said Danny with a grin.

"Well, I did think about taking you there, but resisted the temptation. You can have too much of a good thing."

"Are the boats difficult to steer?" asked Mrs Watson.

"I've never tried," her husband replied, "Some people say they are easier than driving a car, at least you don't need a licence."

They continued to make plans for the holiday and by the time Rachel went home there was a buzz of excitement as they looked forward to a different kind of holiday, but one they knew they would enjoy.

As the twins were going to bed, Karen paused to ask when they could start studying the Beatitudes.

"You finish school next week, so why not the Sunday after?" suggested her mother.

"That's fine with me," agreed her father. "We can then aim to finish by the time you go back to school."

"Typical parents," said Danny. "Talking of going back to school before we even start our holiday."

"Go on," said his father with a twinkle in his eye.

When the children had closed their bedroom doors, Mrs Watson told her husband how pleased she was that even on holiday, the youngsters want to know more about the Bible. With a smile, he agreed.

Karen shares her disappointment

The final week at school passed by very quickly as everyone, teachers included, looked forward to the summer break. Karen, who was very keen on most sports, waited eagerly to see if she had made the first team in her favourite sport, hockey. Although the matches were not until the autumn, the names of those representing the school were to be announced before the holidays.

Danny, on the other hand, was more concerned with his exam results. He had worked hard, but was not very confident in having passed. At least he should hear within a few weeks.

On the day before they broke up, Karen arrived home with a face full of concern.

"Do you want the good news or the bad news first?" she asked her mother who was enjoying a cup of tea whilst reading one of her favourite magazines.

"Try the good news," she replied with an anxious tone in her voice.

"I've been selected to represent the school at hockey next term."

"That's great news," her mother replied with the worry temporarily lifted.

"Now hear the bad news. The first game is to be played on a Sunday."

"I can't believe it."

"Neither could I, but it's true. Some of the other girls aren't happy about it either, because they visit their grandparents on that day. I know they are not Christians and their reason is different to mine, but… Mum, what do I do?"

At this point the front door opened and Mr Watson thankfully arrived home early.

His wife told him the details and waited for his response, with an eye on Karen who was feeling very downcast.

"Karen, I'm sorry to hear of your disappointing news, but we can't sit here and do nothing."

"But Dad, we can't do anything, it's all been arranged."

"We can do something, Karen, even if it doesn't bring the results we want. Tomorrow morning, I'm going to your school to speak to the teacher who is responsible for arranging this event. By the way, what is her name?"

"Oh it's Miss Cartwright, but she won't change her mind," replied Karen annoyed about the whole thing.

"Maybe not, but we'll try," said her father with a confident voice, which for the first time made Karen slightly optimistic. "Don't forget we had the same problem with Danny over his cricket."

The following morning Mr Watson kept his word and met Miss Cartwright at the school. It was a friendly conversation, with Mr Watson being able to share his feelings regarding the Lord's Day and especially how important it was to them as a family. He was assured by Miss Cartwright that the matter would be considered and a reply sent to him as soon as she had discussed it with the schools concerned. Karen was very surprised, but encouraged that the issue was even going to be considered and thanked her father for his help.

Saturday was a busy day. The house was in need of decoration following the extension which was finished last year. Mr Watson wanted to use some of his holidays to at least put the lounge in good order. Mr and Mrs Watson worked hard during the day, but, by Saturday evening they were ready for the day of rest.

Sunday morning began with a bright cloudless sky, but by the time they had returned from church the clouds were gathering. Rachel arrived promptly at 2.30 and within a few minutes everyone was waiting for Mr Watson to introduce the Beatitudes.

"Turn to Matthew chapter 5 and you find nine verses which begin with the word 'Blessed.' We will look at each in turn, but this afternoon let's think about the first verse. Rachel, would you read it please?"

Rachel read the verse slowly and carefully bearing in mind she might have to answer a question about it.

"Has anyone a comment to make on what Rachel has read?" asked Mr Watson.

"It seems like a six point sermon," replied Danny with a big grin.

"Carry on," said his father.

"Well, Jesus saw the multitude; then he went up the mountains; he sat down; his disciples came to him; he opened his mouth and finally he taught them."

"Do I see a young preacher on the horizon?" asked Karen with a serious tone.

Before anyone replied, Mr Watson asked a further question, "Who was Jesus speaking to?"

"Some people say he was talking to his disciples," replied Mrs Watson, "but when the Sermon on the Mount finishes at the end of chapter 7, we are told the people were astonished at his teaching. The disciples may have surrounded him, but others would be listening to his message."

"Can I ask a question?" said Rachel after a brief pause. "Why did Jesus sit to preach?"

"I never thought of that," said Danny looking to his father for help.

Mr Watson began to explain the difference between their culture and ours. In this part of the world it is our custom, when speaking, to sit down when the meeting is informal, such as in a house, or at a picnic. But at the time of Jesus, the religious leaders would stand or walk around as they taught the people. When, however, they had an important message or statement to give, they would sit down.

Mr Watson asked them to turn to Matthew's gospel, [1] where it says Jesus sat in a boat before he told a number of important parables to them. He also took them to another passage [2] where Jesus was sitting on the Mount of Olives before he gave the long statement about the end of the world.

"Yes, but…" interrupted Karen, "these are events that took place outside, but what about inside the synagogue?"

"That's a good point," said Mr Watson. "In the same book of Matthew, 3 Jesus told the disciples that the teachers of the law and the Pharisees sit in Moses' seat. This was a special chair for the town's leading teacher."

"Where was the mountain?" asked Rachel after a short pause to take in what had just been said.

"We don't know exactly," replied Mr Watson. "Some who lived at the time of the early Christian church said it was Mount Tabor, but most believe that it took place on the shores of the Sea of Galilee."

The discussions continued around these verses with the family unaware of the time. Thankfully Lassie was and gave a few sharp barks, reminding Mrs Watson it was time for her tea.

Busy days ahead

"Danny! Karen! It's time I heard some movement up there," shouted their mother. "You can't stay in bed all day." Half an hour later two weary teenagers began to walk slowly downstairs rubbing their eyes and yawning.

"What's for breakfast?" asked Danny making his way to the kitchen.

"Breakfast!" replied his mother. "It's nearly time for lunch."

Danny helped himself to a bowl of cereals and a slice of toast, but Karen who never had much for breakfast drank her usual glass of orange.

"What are your plans this week?" asked their mother.

"We will be spending most of it preparing for the Holiday Bible club at the church," replied Karen. "We've been asked to help with the activity sessions in the afternoon. I have also been asked to go in the mornings to help with the music. Oh, one other thing, I will be at Rachel's tomorrow night to talk about the holidays."

"Well that seems a busy programme. And you young man, what is on your agenda?" asked his mother with a smile.

"I suppose it will be spent mainly eating and sleeping. In between the two I'll be helping Karen prepare for next week. She's asked for some expert advice."

"Cheeky," Karen replied with a chuckle.

The week passed by very quickly. On the Saturday morning Mr and Mrs Watson woke early to hear the noise of rain lashing against their bedroom window.

"That's put an end to my plans for the day," said Mr Watson. "I was hoping to spend some time in the garden before we go on holiday. The lawn will look like a field if I don't cut the grass soon."

"Why not finish the decorating," suggested his wife. "We can then spend some time in the garden next week when the weather hopefully improves."

"Did the wind and rain disturb the children?" asked Mr Watson as he went to the front door to pick up the post.

"It would take an earthquake to disturb them," replied his wife. "Sometimes I'm not sure whether even that would be successful."

It had been a busy day for all the family. Danny and Karen spent most of it at the church making final preparations for the Holiday Bible Club. By six o'clock that evening Mr and Mrs Watson collapsed in the chair worn out from their decorating, but pleased with what had been done.

"Fancy a pizza?" asked Mr Watson after drinking a welcome cup of tea. "It would be here within half an hour."

"I'm too tired to cook," she replied.

When Danny and Karen returned from the church they all tucked in to an enjoyable supper. The rest of the evening was very quiet indeed. Only Lassie managed to keep awake and sometimes that was with a struggle.

Sunday morning began as the previous day with very heavy rain, although from time to time the sun did manage to peep through the clouds.

"I hope the weather improves before our holidays," said Karen. "I don't want to see much water during that fortnight."

"I don't think you will be travelling very far without it." Danny replied with a quick response.

The rain continued throughout the morning, but as they cleared the dishes following dinner, they noticed a gradual improvement. Rachel had joined them for the meal, so it wasn't long before they were ready to begin discussing the first Beatitude.

"Danny will you read the third verse please?" asked his father.

"Blessed are the poor in spirit for theirs is the Kingdom of Heaven."

Mr Watson then began to explain that the Beatitudes were not a set of instructions which a person has to obey to become a Christian, but they showed how a person should live as a Christian. It was important that they as a family should display these qualities at school, at work, in the church and at home.

"So are the Beatitudes just for Christians?" asked Rachel thoughtfully.

"No," replied Mr Watson. "There is a lesson for unbelievers as well because they show people that God is holy, and as we read them we see how sinful we are. We all need to realise the importance of God's holiness and our sinfulness. Now let me move on by asking if anyone can tell me what 'Blessed' means?"

"I know it doesn't mean just being happy," replied Karen, "but I'm not sure what it does mean."

"You are correct with the first statement," said her father to help her out. "The word 'Blessed' does involve happiness, but it means more than that. Any more suggestions?"

"If we are saying that 'blessed' does not mean happy, then are we looking for a word which tells us more about ourselves than our feelings?" asked Mrs Watson hoping she was making herself clear.

"Yes," replied her husband. "When someone is 'blessed' they are not telling us what they feel, but what they are. Happiness comes from inside us, but blessedness comes from God."

"I think I know what you mean," said Danny. "What you are trying to say is that we are not always happy, but we are always blessed. Even when we are sad we are blessed."

"You've got it in one," replied his father.

"I've just been thinking," jumped in Karen a little excitedly.

"Congratulations!" replied Danny.

"I will ignore that comment. My thoughts went to Paul and Silas when they were in prison at Philippi. Although they were in pain after being beaten, they were still able to sing because they were 'blessed' by God."

"That's a good illustration," said her father. "now we will need to move on to the second part. Who are the poor in spirit?"

Everyone remained silent. Mr Watson then began to explain that it does not mean having few things or not much money. Being 'poor in spirit' is when we look into our heart and see nothing but sin and also see how horrible that sin is. We are poor inside and need God to forgive our sin and make us right. It is only when we are poor in a spiritual way that we ask God to forgive us. He will then make us rich in spirit. "I have been thinking again," said Karen turning to Danny to make sure he would make no comment. "If the poor in spirit are those who are poor inside the heart, then that publican in the temple explains what it means when he said 'God be merciful to me a sinner' [4]."

"Exactly right," said her father, "and that leads us to the third point which tells us that these people belong to the Kingdom of Heaven."

"We talked about this matter when we looked at the Lord's Prayer," said Rachel hoping she was right.

"I am pleased someone remembered," said Mr Watson, "but can anyone remember what we said?"

"Can I help out?" suggested Mrs Watson seeing the youngsters' memories were not as good as they thought. "I believe we said that kings have crowns, sceptres and robes which are signs of royalty, but God is King of all Kings and he sits on the throne of heaven. The Kingdom of Heaven is greater than any earthly kingdom and is reserved for all who have put their trust in the Lord Jesus. It is a Kingdom that has great wealth; it is perfect; completely secure, and as Christians it is our future home."

"That's good," said Danny having listened very carefully to all his mother had said. "Thank you Danny. Now will you be good and take Lassie for a quick walk while the girls help me with the tea, because we must beat the clock and be in church on time."

Holiday Bible club

Although the twins were able to lie in last Monday morning, today was different. They had to be at the church by 9 o'clock as this was the first day of the annual Holiday Bible Club.

"Come on Karen, we'll be late," shouted Danny as his sister came out of her bedroom loaded with files and books.

"I'm sorry. I just don't want to forget anything," she replied, feeling a bit tense about it all.

"Don't worry," answered her father, "everything will be fine. I'll take you to the church hall which will save you time."

"Thanks Dad," replied Karen with some relief.

"What time will it finish, so I can come and collect you both?"

"It should be over by 3 o'clock, but we need half an hour to clear up," replied Danny.

When the twins had left the house, their mother made herself a welcome cup of tea, sat down with her Bible and asked God to help all those who would be busy at the church this week. She also prayed that God would speak clearly to the children who attended.

When the twins returned each day, they spent most of the evenings preparing for the following day. Mr and Mrs Watson agreed that they wouldn't ask too many questions until the week had ended, knowing how tired they would be at the end of each day.

The week passed very quickly, and when Danny and Karen walked through the front door on the Friday afternoon, their faces, though tired, were very happy.

"I'm shattered," said Karen dropping all her books on the settee and collapsing beside them.

"Some people just don't have the stamina," said Danny falling into an armchair.

"Wait until you have to work for a living," replied their father as he came into the room. "I've suggested that we have tea a little earlier, so that we can ask you how the week went, that is if you are not too tired."

"It will be your privilege Mr Watson," said Danny with a cheeky grin, "and no, we are not too tired, just worn out."

After tea the family settled into the living room and the twins told their parents what a great week it had been.

"We began with about seventy children," said Karen. "By the end of the week we had over one hundred. During the morning we had a few choruses, quizzes and visual aids. The theme for the week was the story of the Exodus from Egypt which finished with the Children of Israel reaching the Promised Land. We then had the children making models of the story. That was great fun and a bit messy too. It's displayed in the church hall so we hope that people will go and see them."

"And what about you young man?" asked his mother.

"Oh, I helped, but I was responsible for the games in the afternoon. Because the weather was good, we spent most of the time in the field behind the church. I can tell you, when those children went home they looked as we did or probably worse."

Mr and Mrs Watson showed great interest and asked questions, but it was very clear that the week had been a great success and many prayers had been answered.

On the Lord's Day, before the morning service, many parents visited the church hall to see the work which had been done by the children during the previous week. The youth leaders were very encouraged by the comments made by members of the church.

When Rachel arrived after dinner, she also talked excitedly about the week until Mr Watson had to remind them that they had other plans for the afternoon and that was to continue their discussion on the Beatitudes.

When they had settled down, Mr Watson asked his wife if she would read verse four.

"Blessed are those who mourn, for they shall be comforted."

"I want to begin with a question," said Mr Watson. "Is there anything unusual about that first part of the Beatitude?"

After a brief pause, Mr Watson was about to help them, when Rachel made a helpful comment.

"It seems strange that in this sentence there are two words that mean opposite things."

"Carry on," said Mr Watson in an encouraging way.

"Well, we said last week, or was it earlier, that to be blessed was to know God's special favour, and this brings real joy to us. But now we are told that these people mourn. I'm sorry but I don't understand how we can be joyful and yet mourn. Is it just me that has the problem?"

It soon became clear that both Danny and Karen had the same problem.

"What I can't understand," said Danny with a puzzled look on his face, "is when we hear of air crashes when hundreds are killed; when we see war in other parts of the world; when we see suffering through illness and hunger, the words 'blessed' and 'mourn' seem miles apart, but here Jesus brings them together."

"Those comments are honest and helpful, so let's try and see what Jesus is saying to us," replied Mr Watson. "We are told by the media that those who are successful, prosperous, powerful and popular are the happy ones. But are they? The world doesn't like mourners, yet Jesus said that those who mourn are those who know God's blessing."

"Can I jump in here?" asked Karen. "Could it be that the people who look for success and wealth only, will be those who will mourn in eternity, but those who suffer in this life will rejoice in eternity?"

"That is partly true," replied her father. "The apostle Paul helps us here in his letters to Rome [5] and Corinth [6], but I believe the last Beatitude is clearer when we think of grief, suffering and persecution, so we must be careful not to jump too far ahead."

"I have just been reading a very helpful book on the Beatitudes by

John Blanchard," said Mrs Watson who loved reading in her spare time. "He said that there are three kinds of mourning. First there is natural mourning as when someone we love dies. Then there is sinful mourning as we can see in the life of Cain after he killed his brother Abel. Cain was more bothered about himself than what had happened to Abel. Finally, there is spiritual mourning, which the author believes is what Jesus is thinking about in this verse."

"That is very helpful," replied her husband. "The question we now must answer is, what is spiritual mourning?"

"Is it a bit like the first Beatitude?" asked Rachel afraid she might be asked to explain.

"In what way?" asked Mr Watson as predictable as Rachel expected.

"Well, when we talked about being 'poor in spirit', we said it meant to be aware and convicted of our sin. To mourn seems to say we should be sorry and grieve for our sins."

"Rachel, I believe you are right," replied Mr Watson which greatly encouraged her. "Our sins are a great problem to us, and some people even weep over them. They mourn because it was their sins which sent the Saviour to the cross. But Jesus assures us that he will comfort those who mourn."

They continued a little longer until Lassie, who could tell the time better than any of the family, realised she was ready for her tea, and let her feelings be known to everyone.

Prayer is answered

Now that the Holiday Bible Club had finished, the main topic of conversation was the family holiday which was to begin a week on Saturday. There was special excitement as this was the first time anyone had been on a canal boat, so hardly a day passed without it being mentioned.

The postman always arrived early in the morning, and on the Wednesday morning the family had a very encouraging letter.

"Kathy!" her husband shouted from the front room. "A letter has come from the school."

As they opened it they immediately noticed that it was written by Miss Cartwright. They could hardly believe their eyes when they read the contents.

"We must wake up Karen!" said Mrs Watson full of excitement. "On this occasion she'll be pleased to be disturbed from sleep."

It wasn't long before Karen came downstairs with Danny not far behind. He wasn't going to miss anything, especially if it was good news.

"Read this!" said her mother as she handed the letter to her.

Dear Mr Watson,

I am replying following your visit to my office before the end of the school year. You expressed concern over arrangements we made to hold inter-school matches on Sundays.

I received a number of visits and telephone calls from other parents who expressed similar concern, as this was the only day they could spend with their close relations.

After having spoken to the other schools involved, who also received messages of disappointment from parents, it was agreed to re-arrange the fixtures so that the matches will be played sometime during the week or on a Saturday. Further details regarding dates will be given to Karen when she returns in September.

I thought I would write and let you know of our decision as soon as it had been made.

I trust you all have a good holiday.

Yours sincerely

Miss Cartwright

For a moment after the letter had been read there was total silence. Then Karen with great delight flung her arms round her parents necks. Even Danny, to his surprise and slight embarrassment was included.

"I hope these things don't happen often if this is the response," he said with a slight grin. "This is great news," said Mr Watson. "I think we should now thank God for helping us and answering our prayers."

The rest of the week passed by with the main topic being the holidays. Mr and Mrs Watson, however, were aware that there was still much work to be done before they could finally relax.

On the Saturday the sky was clear with warm sunshine, so Mr Watson spent most of the day in the garden, with his wife making sure the home was clean and tidy.

"I have heard people say that meekness is weakness, but this is far from the truth. When you look at some examples of meekness in the Bible you see that the people were strong and full of courage."

As Saturday had been a busy day, the Lord's Day was a very welcome relief. After the morning service some friends wished them a good holiday and looked forward to seeing them again with a good healthy tan.

After dinner, and the dishes washed and put away, coffee was served by Karen and Rachel as the family sat in their usual places in the living room.

"I believe we have now reached verse five," said Mr Watson as

Karen gave him a steaming mug of coffee. "Would you read it Danny?"

"Blessed are the meek for they shall inherit the earth."

"Now before we look at this statement let us remind ourselves of the Beatitudes that we have discussed. Anybody with good memories?"

"The first was poor in spirit," said Danny. "This tells us that without God's presence in our lives we are lost without hope of heaven."

"The second," said Rachel without waiting for anyone to comment on Danny's reply, "is that when we sin we should mourn over it. We should never treat sin lightly, but realise our sin sent Jesus to die on the cross."

After a few more comments which made sure everyone understood and remembered their previous discussion, Mr Watson turned to the third Beatitude.

"What does meek mean?" he asked.

"I tried to spend some time last week looking at the word 'meek'," replied Mrs Watson. "Most translations of the Bible use the word meek, but others use gentle, and humble. In my dictionary it says patient, mild and not angry. I finally decided it takes more than one word to explain it."

"I'm sure you are right," her husband replied, "but let us try to explain it. I have heard people say that meekness is weakness, but this is far from the truth. When you look at some examples of meekness in the Bible you see that the people were strong and full of courage. Can anyone give me an example?"

"Jesus was meek," replied Karen, "at least some hymns say so."

"Yes that's true, but does the Bible say so?" Mr Watson asked.

Everybody knew it did, but couldn't think where. Eventually Mr Watson told them of two verses in Matthew 7 where Jesus is mentioned as being 'meek'.

"Moses was also meek," suggested Mrs Watson. "In Numbers

chapter thirteen verse three we are told he was very meek, but he had to be strong in leading Israel to the Promised Land."

"Those are two good examples that should help us to explain 'meekness', said Mr Watson. "Let us see if we can find some words or sentences that describe this important Beatitude."

"Is 'meekness' one of the fruits of the Spirit?" [8] asked Danny with some hesitation.

"Yes," replied his father. "It can mean gentleness which is a lovely description."

"I think meekness can be humility," said Rachel with some confidence.

"You are doing well," said Mr Watson trying to encourage more replies.

"If someone hurts us or speaks unkindly, the Christian shouldn't get angry or seek to get their own back on them," suggested Mrs Watson.

"I suppose," said Karen, "that meekness is repaying good for evil."

The family continued to find more words to describe meekness, but then Mr Watson asked them to give some reasons why Christians should be meek. A number of suggestions were made, but the most important was given by Rachel who said that we should be meek because it was an example set by Jesus that every Christian should follow.

"Before we finish," said Mr Watson, "we must look at the last part because we are told the meek shall inherit the earth. What does that mean?"

> "The meek shall inherit the earth...Jesus may have been repeating these words to show that although some people are wrongly treated in this life, a calm and patient faith is the most important thing of all. We need to pray that God will send what is best for us, then heaven will make it all complete".

"I know what inherit means," replied Danny. "It is to possess something that has been given or left to you. I suppose the Children of Israel inherited the land of Canaan, because they possessed what God had given to them."

Mr Watson gave them time to think about those last words, then he asked them to turn to Psalm 37:11 where David says 'the meek shall inherit the earth'. He said that Jesus may have been repeating these words to show that although some people are wrongly treated in this life, a calm and patient faith is the most important thing of all. Some may inherit wealth, but contentment with what we have is the greatest blessing of all. We need to pray that God will send to us now on earth what is best for us, then heaven will make it all complete.

It's here at last

The following Wednesday morning Mr Watson received an unexpected letter. It came from the local Magistrates Court asking him to be available for jury service in October. "How do you feel about it?" asked his wife looking slightly anxious.

"I think it will be an interesting experience," he replied. "Yes, I think I will look forward to it, although you can't be sure of being on a jury. I know of some people who have sat in the waiting room for hours without entering the courtroom. Anyway we'll have to wait and see. At least it is after the holidays."

Mr and Mrs Watson were very busy during Thursday and Friday making sure everything was ready so they could leave as early as possible on the Saturday morning. The weather had been cloudy during the early part of the week, but when Saturday came the sun was shining from a clear blue sky. Rachel had stayed with the Watsons on the Friday night so there was no delay in leaving the next day. Everyone was excited at breakfast time; even Lassie knew something different was happening.

"Don't forget the camera," shouted Karen to Danny who was coming out of his bedroom.

"Don't worry, and I have plenty of films as well."

"What's that you are carrying?" asked Rachel as Danny came downstairs.

"It's a file. I have decided to write details with photos of each day of the holiday. Perhaps one day it may become a popular book entitled 'Danny Watson's Diary.'"

Mr Watson made sure that everybody's case was in the hall before loading them into the car. He then checked that all the windows and back door were closed and locked.

"Has everyone got everything they need, because soon it will be too late?"

"Sure Dad, everything is present and correct," replied Danny with a salute.

Mr Watson then gave a brief prayer asking God to give them a safe journey and a very happy holiday together. Within minutes they were on their way heading for the Midlands.

On the journey, Mr Watson told them that they would begin at Evesham and travel on the Avon ring which would take them through Stratford-upon-Avon and Worcester. They would cover 109 miles and go through 131 locks sailing on both the River Avon and the Severn.

"That sounds a little bit like hard work to me," said Danny when he thought of all those locks to get through.

"Well we can go round the Thames ring which is 252 miles long and goes through 175 locks," replied his father.

"I think we should stick to your first plan," Danny finally decided.

Eventually they arrived at Evesham Marina after a very enjoyable journey. The boat would be ready at 4pm so they decided to park the car and give Lassie a good run before they returned. As they walked beside the canal and saw the narrow bridges that their boat would have to go through, Karen and Rachel were a little worried, but Mr Watson seemed very calm, so they decided to put their fears to the back of their mind.

When they arrived back at the Marina the boat was ready. After Mr Watson had been given instructions, the family put the cases on board and then started to unpack. It was a colourful boat with two double and two single bedrooms; a beautiful kitchen and a large lounge.

"We are not going too far tonight," said Mr Watson when the unpacking had been done. "I have been told there is a beautiful, quiet area to moor the boat for tomorrow and a church near the canal."

They all slept well that first night and woke to a warm sunny morning. When they returned from church they had some lunch and then sat in the open to begin their discussion on the fourth Beatitude.

"Will you read it Rachel?"

"Blessed are those who hunger and thirst for righteousness, for they shall be filled."

"Can anyone tell me what is different between the first three beatitudes and this one?" asked Mr Watson.

There was silence as everyone looked carefully at the words in their Bibles. It was Mrs Watson who was the first to speak.

"When Jesus spoke about the poor; those who mourn; and the meek he was describing what people are. Now he is telling the disciples what people **do**—and here they hunger and thirst."

"That's a good comment," her husband replied. "Now let's look at the words 'hunger' and 'thirst'."

"When you are hungry, it is a sign that you are alive."

"I'm sorry, I don't understand," replied Rachel with a puzzled look on her face.

"Let me try and explain," said Mrs Watson. "When Danny and Karen were born they were immediately hungry, and that was a sign that they were alive. Someone who is dead cannot be hungry."

"Oh, I see what you mean. It is fairly obvious isn't it? Sorry for being so stupid."

"Perish the thought," said Danny with a grin on his face.

"Can I say something else?" asked Rachel eagerly. "If a baby is hungry as soon as it is born, then we should be spiritually hungry when we become Christians. You can say when we are born again."

"You have hit the nail right on the head," said Mr Watson. "Well done."

They began to look in the Psalms at verses which talk about the need for spiritual thirst. Verses such as Psalm 42: 1-2 and Psalm 63:1 were mentioned.

> "Before they prayed, Mr Watson tied all their thoughts together by saying how important it was to hunger and thirst for the things of God. It showed we were spiritually alive and healthy. After all, when we do this, Jesus promises that we shall be satisfied."

"Let me ask another question," suggested Mr Watson. "I said that hunger and thirst was a sign of life, but is it a sign of anything else?"

"When I was ill a few years ago," replied Karen, "I went with Mum to the doctor's and she asked me if I had lost my appetite. I suppose that something is wrong when we don't want food, but we are getting better when we are hungry again."

"So that means that hunger shows we are healthy," said Danny supporting his sister.

"That's right," said his father. "Now although this Beatitude is not as difficult to explain as some of the others, tell me what will keep us spiritually alive and healthy."

"Reading the Bible," said Karen, "and talking about it as we are doing today."

"We should also pray," suggested Rachel. "If we enjoy talking with one another we should look forward to talking with God even more."

"Going to church," said Danny determined not to be left out.

"Which reminds me," interrupted Mrs Watson, "that we should be getting ready for doing exactly that."

Before they prayed, Mr Watson tied all their thoughts together by saying how important it was to hunger and thirst for the things of God. It showed we were spiritually alive and healthy. After all, when we do this, Jesus promises that we shall be satisfied.

Stormy weather

It was just after 7am when Mr and Mrs Watson heard a knock on their bedroom door. "Come on, get up! It's a beautiful day," shouted Danny.

"Why can't you lie in, we're on holiday," replied his mother. "You get breakfast ready and we'll be with you in half an hour."

After a relaxing breakfast, which was always followed with a Bible reading and prayers, the family began to prepare for the next stage of their journey. Before they departed Mr Watson explained to the youngsters how to steer the boat. He told them it was the opposite of driving a car, as with the boat you steer from the back and if you want to turn right you have to pull to the left. He then showed them how the lock gates opened as he would need their help in getting through. He also warned them that the boat had no brakes, so if you wanted to stop you would slow down and put the engines in reverse. It seemed a bit complicated at first but by the end of the day, they were becoming experts at it. They set targets each day so they could be sure to be back at Evesham in ten days time. Mr Watson aimed to cover 20 miles each day which was a good distance as the boat only travelled at 4 miles per hour.

The first three days passed by without a problem and the weather was sunny and warm. On the Thursday afternoon it became humid with dark clouds gathering.

"I think we are in for a storm," said Mr Watson as he looked towards the west from where the clouds were coming.

It wasn't long before thunder was heard and Lassie ran as fast as her legs could carry her under the table.

"She will be alright," said Mrs Watson "as long as we are not too far away."

"There's one thing about a canal boat," said Rachel, "you can't be too far away."

8

Soon the rain fell making a loud noise on the roof of the boat. Then came the lightning.

"I don't know whether I'm enjoying this," said Karen looking for some sympathy.

"Don't worry, I think it will soon be over," replied her mother confidently.

"Look at the lightning, it's terrific," said Danny with his face against the window.

"I believe you," said his sister with her face firmly into a cushion.

Within an hour the main storm had passed and all they could hear was the rain bouncing on the roof.

"I've a suggestion to make," said Mr Watson. "We can't go anywhere tonight as it's still raining, so why don't we get something to eat and then discuss the next Beatitude."

Very soon the smell of a mixed grill began to waft round the boat and by 6 o'clock they were tucking into a very welcome meal. As Mrs Watson had done the main work in preparing the meal, the youngsters agreed to wash the dishes and make the kitchen tidy. It wasn't long before they were ready for Mr Watson to read the fifth Beatitude.

> "God has been especially merciful to us and others in sending Jesus Christ to be our Saviour. Let us thank God that He has been merciful which means we should be merciful to others."

"Blessed are the merciful, for they shall obtain mercy. Now this is one of the shortest Beatitudes, but it has much to teach us," continued Mr Watson. "We must always remember that these statements of Jesus do not show us how to be saved but show what a real Christian is like. Another mistake we shouldn't make is to choose some instructions, and then by obeying them think we are pleasing God."

"What I think you are saying," interrupted Karen, "is that we don't become Christians by obeying the Beatitudes, but when we are Christians we live by the teaching of Jesus."

"That's exactly right," replied her father. "Also remember that this Beatitude begins with a duty, but ends with a reward."

"What does being merciful mean?" asked Rachel who was keen to get to the subject they were to discuss.

"I looked it up in the dictionary," replied Danny, "and it used words like 'kindness', and 'compassion'. Is that right?"

His father began to explain that Christians should have compassion for the needs and sufferings of other people. We should be greatly concerned by the misery and unhappiness that others are facing. Sin has brought these things upon many people throughout the world, but sadly we are so often unmoved by it all.

"Jesus wasn't," said Mrs Watson. "He had compassion on people because they were like sheep without a shepherd, [9] but he did something about it. He fed the hungry and healed the sick. He felt pity for those in need."

"I suppose it's not just being concerned" said Karen, "but doing something about it."

"Let us turn to the first letter of John [10]," suggested Mr Watson, "and we will see that Karen's thoughts are right. The apostle asks how the love of God can be in a person who has possessions, and yet does not give to his brother who is in need. He also says later on [11] that if a person does not love his brother whom he has seen, he cannot love God whom he has not seen. The apostle James [12] says that faith without deeds is of little value. There are some people who are good on Bible teaching but poor on giving. The Christian should be a generous person."

"Are we then just to show mercy by giving to those who are in need?" asked Danny.

"No," replied his mother. "We are to show mercy to those who ask for forgiveness. Do you remember when we looked at the Lord's

Prayer and the verse that tells us to forgive those who hurt us in many different ways?"

"So do we show mercy hoping that we will be shown mercy by others?" asked Danny.

"Not exactly," replied his mother. "That misses the point. We are to show mercy because God has shown mercy to us."

"It goes back to the Lord's Prayer" said Rachel. "We are to forgive, because we are forgiven by God."

"Exactly," replied Mrs Watson, pleased that they all understood.

"Have you noticed the rain has stopped?" asked Mr Watson.

Because everyone was involved in the discussions nobody had realised the storm had passed and the clouds had departed.

"We will close in a moment, but before we do, just remember that God is merciful to all people in that He sends the rain and sunshine. He also gives us so much to enjoy. Think of the beautiful countryside we have seen already. But more important than that, He has been especially merciful to us and others in sending Jesus Christ to be our Saviour. Let us thank God that He has been merciful which means we should be merciful to others."

Problems with pleasures

"**D**o you realise a week has nearly gone by?" asked Danny as they continued along the River Severn passing the city of Worcester.

"I hear that Yorkshire are playing cricket at the county ground this week," said Mr Watson wearing his white rose hat to protect him from the sun.

"No cricket matches on holiday," said Mrs Watson firmly.

"Make the boat go as fast as you can until we have passed Worcester," said Karen to Danny.

"I'm doing my best," replied her brother, pretending he had sweat dripping from his forehead.

A few hours later as the family were relaxing, Karen suddenly saw swans with a young family.

"Look over here!" she shouted. "Aren't they beautiful?"

They carefully counted twenty two young signets swimming without a care in the world.

"Don't the parents look proud?" said Rachel. "Danny, please pass my camera."

"Look over there," said Danny eagerly as some herons stood on the other side of the canal. "The place seems full of wildlife." Again more photographs were taken.

The afternoon passed by very quickly, but as Mrs Watson and Rachel were preparing the evening meal, suddenly, the engine cut out. Mr Watson tried the starter motor, but it wouldn't work. Fortunately the meal was nearly ready so the family began to eat while Mr Watson searched for his mobile telephone to ring the boat company. Later that evening a mechanic arrived and discovered that the fuel valve had split.

"I can't repair it now," he said. "I'll be back in about two hours."

He kept exactly to his word and eventually the problem was put right.

"Well we can't go much further, and with it being the Lord's Day tomorrow we will find a good place to tie the boat against the bank," suggested Mr Watson.

When they finally got the boat beside the bank, Danny suddenly realised that the ropes which held the boat were on the other side. They tried to get hold of the ropes but Rachel was accidentally pulling one around Karen's legs which nearly threw her into the water.

Immediately everyone became concerned for Karen, but it was Danny who relieved the tension.

"I have been trying to do that for years," he said. Soon everybody including Karen saw the funny side of it.

"I'm glad I had my camera," said Danny so loud that all could hear.

"I'll get my own back," replied Karen, "fear not my dear brother."

"I'm afraid she might be right," said his father with a smile.

On the Lord's Day morning they found a church within walking distance of the canal. Although the service was a little different to their own, the message had been helpful to them. After they had eaten, the family sat along the edge of the boat ready to continue their discussion.

"Could you read the next verse Karen?" asked her father.

"Blessed are the pure in heart, for they shall see God."

"This is one of the clearest and greatest statements Jesus made," said Mr Watson. "To try and discover what Jesus meant we have to find some key words. Any suggestions?"

"I can see two," replied Danny. "What about the words 'heart' and 'pure'?"

"I have noticed another word," said Rachel eagerly. "The word 'see' is important."

"That's good," said Mr Watson. "Now let's see what these words mean. First of all we must look at the heart. What is the heart as far as the Bible is concerned?"

"Our emotions come from the heart," replied Mrs Watson.

"In Psalm 28 verse 7 the writer said his heart leapt for joy. Then in Psalm 73 verse 21 he said his heart was grieved."

"That's very helpful," replied her husband. "Now I have noticed a verse in Psalm 23 which gives another emotion which comes from the heart."

"I've got it!" shouted Danny. "It's verse 3 where he says his heart shall not fear."

"Well done!" said Mr Watson. "So the emotion of joy, grief and fear all come from the heart."

"I've got another," said Rachel, "but I can't remember where it's from. Jesus said that we are to love God with all our heart." [13]

"That's good." Mr Watson replied. "It would have been a mistake to miss the emotions of love. What else comes from the heart?"

"Evil thoughts," said Karen gloomily.

"I'm afraid so" replied her father. "The Bible tells us that the heart is very wicked. Jesus told the religious teachers that they had evil thoughts in their hearts [14] The Bible also tells us that God will judge the thoughts of our hearts. [15]"

"Faith also comes from the heart," suggested Mrs Watson. "I think it is in Romans chapter 10 verse 10 that Paul says we believe with our heart."

"That's all very helpful," said Mr Watson, "but we must not miss one other point and that is God sees our heart and knows our thoughts. Let's look at the second word 'pure'. Has anyone any suggestions to make?"

"Christians can see God in two ways. We can see Him in a spiritual sense... when we know Him, we can see Him with our spiritual eyes. For example we can see Him in Creation, for He made everything, and we praise Him for this".

"When I think of things that are pure," said Rachel, "I think of things that are perfect and clean, but that worries me a bit, because my heart and my thoughts are not perfect."

"That's a very good point to make," replied Mr Watson. "A pure heart does not mean a perfect heart. If it did none of us would see God, because all people are sinners. The apostle John says that if we claim to be without sin we are not truthful."[16]

Mr Watson then continued to explain to them that the promises in the Bible were not for those who think they are perfect, but for those who want to be holy and pure. He told them that God dwells in the heart therefore it must be holy, and as all our actions come from the heart, we must be careful what we do, think and say. A person with a pure heart does not knowingly sin, but hates it, because it was sin which sent Jesus to the cross. If God hates it, so should we.

"Now, let us look at the final word," suggested Mr Watson. "What does it mean to see God?"

"I have a problem," said Danny.

"We know," said Karen cheekily.

"Well, let's see if we can help you," replied his father.

"It says in the Bible, that no man has seen God at any time, so how can we see Him?"

"I know this sounds difficult," said his father with care, "but Christians can see God in two ways. We can see Him in a spiritual sense. What I mean is that when we know Him, we can see Him with our spiritual eyes. For example we can see Him in Creation, for He made everything, and we praise Him for this. Can we see God in other things?"

"We can see God in the Bible," said Karen beginning to understand what her father was trying to say to them.

"We can see him when we pray," said Rachel.

"That's right," said Mr Watson. "Although we can't see him with the eyes we have now, yet we can know he is with us. There are many other ways we can see him with spiritual eyes and we can discuss these later, but the most wonderful thing of all is that the Christians shall see God face to face." [17]

"It's hard to understand that one day we shall look at Him, just as I can look at Karen or anyone here," said Rachel with a sparkle in her eyes.

"Whatever experience we have now will be nothing compared with the fact that one day we will see Him," said Mrs Watson.

"I have just been thinking," said Karen. "You know Mrs Peterson at church who is nearly blind? She will see him clearly. It's so exciting to think that one day every Christian will look at Jesus face to face."

"It sure is" said Mr Watson with a smile.

The boat gets trapped

"How is your diary filling up Danny?" asked Rachel as they tucked into their cereals and toast. "I have decided to buy a folder and write out each day's events with the photos I've taken. It should look good when it's done. The only problem is the size of the folder as I have more information than I expected."

"Come on, let's clear up and put everything away safely, and then we can get on our way," said Mrs Watson eagerly. "Now the thunderstorm has passed it looks like being a warm and sunny day."

"...they tucked into their cereals and toast..."

They had been travelling a few hours when Mr Watson noticed a big bend with a bridge immediately after.

"Can we get round?" asked Karen.

Unfortunately as they tried to get the boat round the bend and lined up to meet the bridge, the back of the boat hit the bank, and decided to remain there. Mr Watson and Danny struggled for nearly half an hour to free the boat using long poles to push against the bank. Suddenly it bounced free and they were able to continue through the bridge, a little embarrassed that a number of other boats had been held up.

During the afternoon they travelled through some beautiful countryside with very attractive thatched cottages beside the canal. Both Danny and Rachel were busy taking photographs while Mr and Mrs Watson kept their eyes open for the many kinds of wildlife that could be seen along the bank.

Not only were the youngsters enjoying the holiday, so was Lassie. She would run alongside the canal with Danny, and on one occasion jumped from the bank onto the boat. She was having a marvellous time.

"Hasn't the holiday gone by quickly?" asked Mrs Watson as they were having their evening meal. "Just think only three more days to go and we'll be home."

"Yes, but it's been good and I'm sure we all feel better for it," replied her husband. "We should try and plan the last two days so we are near the marina on Friday night."

"I know I'm not a fan of Shakespeare," said Danny, "but could we see Stratford-upon-Avon?"

"I was hoping we could finish there tomorrow evening and then on to Evesham the following day," replied his father. "Can I suggest that as it is not too late, and we all seem to lack physical energy, why not use some of our mental energy and consider the next Beatitude?"

It wasn't long before Mrs Watson was reading the ninth verse.

"Blessed are the peacemakers, for they shall be called the sons of God."

"We now come to the seventh step on the ladder," said Mr Watson. "Notice the link with this Beatitude and the previous one. The book of James tells us that wisdom is first pure and then peaceable. [18] Jesus also joins them together. I would say this Beatitude is accepted by most people, even those who aren't Christians."

"Is that why we hear of well-known people, especially politicians, who try to make peace agreements between nations who are at war?" asked Danny.

"Yes that's right," replied his father. "When the political upheaval began in Northern Ireland in the 1970's and 1980's a peace movement was formed. Leaders in our own country and America have tried to bring peace in the Middle East between Jews and Arabs for many years. Throughout history since the time of Noah there have been wars and violence—you even read of them in many books of the Bible."

"I read recently that 30 million people were killed during the first World War," said Mrs Watson. "After the war ended 58 countries signed a peace agreement, yet in the second World War over 90 million people died."

"It frightens me," said Rachel, "that countries have so many weapons that can kill millions of people."

"Yes, and we even sell them to our enemies to make money," added Danny.

"I agree with what you say, " said his father, "but remember war begins when love turns to hatred, and it can happen in a small way which in time grows out of control. It can even begin in families, and brings a great deal of unhappiness."

"So what is the problem and how does it begin?" asked Karen.

"I'm afraid Karen, it is the problem of the heart," replied her mother. "Our hearts can be so wicked, and greedy. The book of James tells us that war often comes because people want their own way. [19] It is in the heart where the problem is found and it will never be solved until the heart is made pure."

"That's right," agreed Mr Watson. "Only Christians can be true peacemakers. Remember these are the people Jesus is talking to. If Christians can't be peacemakers, then who can?"

"I've just been thinking" said Rachel, uncertain of how to express her thoughts, "If we are to be like God and Jesus, then we are to be peacemakers. God our Father is the God of Peace [20], and Jesus our Saviour is the Prince of Peace [21]."

"Very good," said Mr Watson, "but what about the Holy Spirit because he is the Spirit of Peace."

"Also remember," said Mrs Watson, "that Jesus prayed for peace and died for it." [22]

"Can I say something else?" asked Rachel.

"Yes, go on," encouraged Mr Watson.

"If we had peace in our families, in our churches and in our country, wouldn't it be great?"

"I am sure we would all agree with that," replied Mr Watson. "It is so important that Christians are never troublemakers but peace-makers."

"So if our heart is pure," said Karen, "we will be careful what we say so that we don't hurt anyone."

"That's right," replied her mother, "but I would take it a little further. Be careful what you say, but also what you think, do and hear. I am sure that if we do this, we are going a long way in obeying these words of Jesus."

Back home again

"Hasn't God been good to us?" said Mrs Watson as they prepared for the next stage of the journey. "Not only have we had a good time and seen some beautiful scenery, but the weather has been perfect."

Mr Watson told them that within an hour they would be travelling along an aqueduct. The canal at that point would be very narrow with only a few inches of water either side of the boat.

As they came toward the aqueduct, they could see traffic travelling beneath them. Lassie who didn't want to miss anything, put her paws on the side of the boat trying to see what was beneath her.

"Lassie, this is not the time to jump," said Danny as he took a firm hold of her collar.

"That was brilliant," said Karen as they reached the other side. "I wish we could do that again."

"No way," replied Rachel. "I hate heights especially when I am so close to the edge."

"They continued through woodland scenery until Karen noticed they were coming into a busy area.

"Is this Stratford-upon-Avon?" she asked.

"Sure is," replied her father.

"It's nearly as bad as Clapham Junction, but on water. What a sight! Just look at all those boats of every size. Where do we put ours?" she asked her father.

"I'm not sure," he replied looking carefully for a good place to tie the boat.

"There's a place here!" shouted Danny.

"Well done lad!" he replied. "I think we can just about get it between those other boats, but it will be tight."

Eventually the boat was fastened securely and they spent the afternoon visiting the World of Shakespeare; Anne Hathaway's

Cottage and especially the Teddy Bear Museum where Mrs Watson, Karen and Rachel stayed as long as possible. Mr Watson and Danny sensibly kept their thoughts to themselves.

"Where is the Royal Shakespeare Theatre?" asked Karen as they returned to the boat late that afternoon.

"You can hardly miss it," said her mother pointing to a building opposite where they tied the boat. "Come on. I'm ready for my tea and my legs need a rest."

The evening passed quietly with the family talking about the events of the day.

The final day saw them returning to the marina for their final evening in Evesham.

The following morning Mr Watson thanked the owners of the boat and with the family made their way to where they parked the car.

"Well I hope you have enjoyed the fortnight," said Mr Watson as they travelled home on the motorway.

"It's been brilliant," said Danny, and all agreed.

It was good to be home even though the holiday had gone so well. The following day, after the morning service, many friends asked them about the holiday; by looking at the colour of their faces they knew that at least the weather had been good.

Following, dinner Rachel joined them. Soon after she arrived, the rain began to fall—but after the hot weather, it was very welcome.

"Are you ready?" asked Mr Watson as they settled back into more comfortable chairs than they had been used to during the past fortnight.

"Would you read the tenth verse?" asked Mr Watson looking towards his wife.

"Blessed are those who are persecuted for righteousness' sake, for theirs is the kingdom of heaven."

"Thank you," he replied. "Now this verse is very different from the other Beatitudes. The seven we have discussed shows what comes from within us, such as meekness, peace and mercy. This one shows what can happen to us as Christians. Are you following me?"

"Yes," replied Rachel. "If we live as God wants us to live, we'll have problems such as being teased and laughed at. I sometimes have this at school."

"The world in which we live," said Mr Watson, "is against all that Jesus taught, so if we stand up for Jesus, opposition will come."

For a short time they read some stories in the Old and New Testaments of believers who were persecuted for their faith, sometimes physically. They began in Genesis where Cain murdered righteous Abel, and looked at many examples.

"If we live as God wants us to live, we will have problems such as being teased and laughed at. I sometimes have this at school."

"Sometime ago," remembered Danny, "I read a book about Christians who a few hundred years ago suffered in this country. Some were burned to death which sounds horrible."

"Yes, it's not easy to read these books," said his mother, "but I believe children of your age need to be aware of what Christians went through to give us freedom today. The biggest danger is forgetting."

"Do you remember" asked Karen, "when those missionaries came to our church and talked about the sufferings of Christians in countries that are not Christian? He showed us some photographs and slides and asked us to pray for them."

"Yes I do," replied Danny, "and this is happening today not centuries ago."

"And we don't find time to pray for them as we should be doing," interrupted Rachel.

The family usually prayed at the end of their discussions, but Mr Watson felt they should stop at this point and pray for missionaries and Christians they knew who were suffering for their faith.

"It seems strange," said Karen, "that those who suffer for their faith are called blessed."

"It does," replied their mother, "but these people remember who they are suffering for, and that is Jesus."

"They also remember" said Mr Watson, "that Jesus had suffered for them. And I am sure they look forward to the future when they would suffer no more, and be with Jesus for ever in heaven."

"Isn't it encouraging," suggested Mrs Watson, "to think that those who carry a cross now, because that is what Jesus told us to do, will one day have their reward. We need to remember that in case we have to suffer for Jesus."

"I think that's a good thought to end on," said Mr Watson, as he finished with a prayer.

Chapter 11

Burglars visit the Watsons

"Danny it's for you," shouted his mother as he was in the bathroom trying to wake himself up under the shower. "I think it's your exam results."

It wasn't long before he was dressed and bounding down the stairs two at a time.

"You seem very eager," said his father.

Danny carefully opened the envelope with a serious look on his face. He read through the details carefully, but as he did so a faint smile began to turn to a grin.

"Brilliant!" he said throwing the paper into the air which landed on Lassie's nose.

"Well done!" said his parents as they took careful note of the results. "You worked hard, so you deserve the credit."

"Hasn't Karen got her results?" asked Danny.

"They should have come this morning; I hope they'll be here tomorrow," replied his mother. "Karen met the postman, but when she found there was no letter, she decided to take Lassie for a walk."

On the Tuesday morning, Karen did receive her results. Although her parents were pleased with them, Karen was expecting better grades so she was slightly disappointed.

During the afternoon, the family had received an invitation to supper at some friends who also belonged to their church. Most of the evening was taken up with conversation about the holidays, but Danny made sure that his exam results were not forgotten.

When they returned home, Mr Watson noticed the side gate into the garden was open and he was sure he left it closed.

"Wait in the car a moment while I check everything is OK"

He walked around the back of the house and to his dismay a window had been forced open and the back door was swinging in the strong wind. He checked that no-one was still around then returned to the car.

"I think we've had unwanted visitors," he said as the family waited for his return. "I'll ring the police, but don't touch anything until they've been."

They went carefully inside making sure that nothing was touched.

They went carefully inside making sure that nothing was touched...Mr Watson's computer had gone.

They noticed that drawers had been removed from dressing tables; wardrobe doors had been left open and Mr Watson's computer had gone. Although everything looked untidy, there was no damage to the furniture or the walls and doors.

"I'll get it" said Danny as the door bell rang.

The police arrived, and after saying how sorry they were, began to ask questions while another officer looked for fingerprints.

"Are you aware of any items that are missing?" asked a tall police officer with a well trimmed moustache.

"My husband's computer has been taken, and I've noticed a few items of jewellery missing. We also had a few antiques which had been handed down by our Grandparents, and they seem to have gone. The worst thing is to realise that somebody has been in your home and touched things that belong to you."

"I understand," he replied. "It's even happened to me. Are you insured?"

"Oh yes," Mrs Watson replied. "My husband will be contacting them in the morning."

The family spent the remainder of the week getting the house back to normal. By the Saturday afternoon, the house was almost back to normal with the window and door repaired.

After the events of the week, they welcomed the Lord's Day with a sense of relief, for they were ready for a break.

As they met for their discussion in the afternoon, Mrs Watson read verse eleven which said, 'Blessed are you when they revile and persecute you, and say all kinds of evil against you falsely for my sake.'

"Now some people finish the Beatitudes at verse ten, but I want to end at verse twelve, so next week will be our last discussion."

"But isn't verse eleven similar to verse ten?" asked Rachel, a little unsure if she was right or wrong. "I mean, it talks about persecution in both verses."

"It is similar," replied Mr Watson, "but it is also different.

Persecution is not just a physical thing—we can cause people to suffer by the things we say. Often people say things that hurt and are untrue."

"I read recently," said Mrs Watson, "that persecution can be in the form of slander as well as slaughter. They said the tongue can hurt more than the sword."

"Dad, you said a minute ago that things hurt us when they are untrue" remembered Karen. "Well, I think the important word is 'falsely', because that is the opposite of untrue."

> "Persecution is not just a physical thing—we can cause people to suffer by the things we say. Many times people say things that hurt and are untrue."

"Well done," said her father. "It is very serious when people say something which is false which damages a person's reputation. Can anyone think of people who have suffered because they have become a Christian?"

Mrs Watson told them of a friend whose son was involved with a gang. When he became a Christian, he knew he was asking for trouble from the rest of the gang, but he stood firm even though he was threatened for it. Rachel also knew someone who became a Christian, but her parents made her life at home very difficult and unhappy. They said she wouldn't keep it up.

"We must remember," said Mr Watson, "that not only ungodly gangs or parents become angry when someone close to them becomes a Christian, but so is the devil. He doesn't like to lose anybody."

"I do find it difficult sometimes," confessed Rachel, "when people at school say unkind and untrue things about me. My parents are very kind to me and I have friends at the church, but when I am by myself at school it isn't always easy."

"I know how you feel," said Mrs Watson in a sympathetic voice.

"Remember we were teenagers once and it can be hard, but God does help us and so will your friends."

"We must mention the last three words," said Mr Watson looking at his watch and realising time was going by quickly. "The words 'for my sake' are very important. It tells us that the Christian is blessed when persecuted for the sake of Jesus. Our Saviour makes it clear that it has to be because of this. If the world hates us, remember, it hated him first."

"Can I have the last word?" asked Danny.

"Sure, go on," replied his father.

"If Jesus suffered on the cross to take away my sin, then I hope he will help me to suffer for him."

Joy overcomes suffering

"Danny!" shouted Mrs Watson, "can you and Karen take Lassie for a run in the park before tea? Your father will be back home from work within the hour and I haven't even thought about dinner."

"Come on girl, get your lead," said Danny.

Lassie loved being free to run in the park. She also loved to swim across the river, but wasn't very popular when she shook the water out of her coat.

"What's matter with her Danny?" asked Karen as she saw Lassie limping towards them.

"Oh, no!" said Danny as he lifted her paw and saw a nasty deep cut across her pad.

"Where did she get that from?" asked Karen as she made her way to the area where she first saw Lassie limping.

"What idiots could have done that!" said Danny as he came across glass bottles which had been broken against a tree. "I could strangle them."

"Calm down," said Karen. "Lassie needs our help."

He picked up the dog in his arms after covering her paw with a handkerchief, and they ran home as fast as possible.

"Mum!" said Karen as she opened the door with Danny close behind. "Lassie has cut her paw on a broken bottle."

"I can see that," replied her mother as she looked at the blood-stained handkerchief. A careful examination revealed that it would be best if she was taken immediately down to the vet.

"You stay here Karen and tell your father where we are when he returns from work. Come on Danny, let's try and get some attention to her paw. I'll just ring the vet and tell her we are coming."

An hour later they returned with a dog looking very sorry for herself and a well bandaged paw containing two stitches.

"I'm sorry dinner will be late," said Mrs Watson to her husband after briefly explaining the events of the afternoon. "You also look sorry for yourself. Is everything all right?"

"Yes fine," replied her husband. "Well, to be honest it's not been an easy day. There's a young man in the office who's been promoted to a better position with an increase in salary. An older man was expecting to get it and has taken the news badly. I suppose I've been putting into practice verse nine, and trying to be a peacemaker. Things will settle down, but it was a bit tense today."

> **If we ever face suffering...we grow closer to God, and our faith becomes stronger. If we are never tested we remain weak. Trials make us stronger."**

On the Thursday morning, Danny received a parcel through the post containing his holiday photographs. He was very pleased with them and could hardly wait to show them to his parents when they returned home.

"They have come out very well," said his mother as they went through them later that day.

Many of them showed the beautiful countryside, but there were times when they had a good laugh, especially when they saw a picture of Karen almost falling into the canal. The photos brought back many memories of an enjoyable holiday.

"Well," said Mr Watson as they sat in the front room after a very satisfying Sunday dinner. "This will be our last discussion on the Beatitudes, so let's make the most of our time together. Can you read verse twelve Rachel?"

"Rejoice and be exceeding glad, for great is your reward in heaven, for so persecuted they the prophets who were before you."

Before Mr Watson could say anything about this verse Rachel continued speaking.

"I have to say that I find it difficult to see how people can rejoice when they are persecuted. I don't think I would."

"I'm not so sure either," added Danny.

"That's a fair comment," replied Mr Watson, "I think I would have felt the same at your age. Let us see if we feel any different at the end, and try and remember what we said when we looked at verse ten. When we began the Beatitudes we said that most people think they are happy when they are prosperous, powerful or popular. The Christian rejoices because he is a child of God. Now, can you think of any reasons why we should rejoice as Christians, and don't think at this point about persecution?"

"Because Jesus has forgiven our sins," answered Karen confidently.

"That's right," replied her father. "Any more?"

"We can now talk to our Creator," said Danny.

"The Holy Spirit directs our lives and helps us to make wise decisions," said Mrs Watson.

"There is at least one more reason that you've missed," suggested Mr Watson, "and it's in the verse Rachel read."

They were all ready to give the answer, but Karen was first to remind them that they should rejoice because they have a great reward in heaven.

"Now let me ask another question," said Mr Watson. "Can you think of reasons why we should rejoice even when we have to face suffering?"

"The only way our sins could be forgiven," said Mrs Watson, "was for Jesus to suffer. He faced great persecution, and we are told to take up our cross and follow Him. Was it Peter [23] who told Christians to rejoice when you share in Christ's sufferings?"

"That's right," her husband replied. "I read recently about John Wesley who travelled many miles on horseback in the eighteenth century. When he was preaching, stones and rotten eggs were thrown at him, but he was willing to suffer, because Jesus suffered for him."

"When it mentioned the prophets," said Danny, "I also thought of

Chapter 12

Elijah and Daniel and many others who were willing to suffer for their faith."

"So if we have to suffer or face persecution, we are in good company," suggested Karen.

"I couldn't have put it better myself," replied her father. "There is another reason why we should rejoice if we ever face suffering, and that is that we grow closer to God, and our faith becomes stronger. If we are never tested we remain weak. Trials make us stronger."

"I suppose," said Rachel, "that if we made a list of our sufferings and a list of our joys, the second list would easily win."

"I'm sure that all our problems and trials will be worth it all when we see Jesus."

"Danny," said his father, "to hear you say that, makes these discussions worthwhile."

Mrs Watson then reminded her husband that they had been invited by Mr and Mrs Edwards for tea, so they should begin to get ready.

"Before I go," said Rachel, "I want to thank you for being so kind and helping me to understand more about God and the teaching of Jesus. I do feel I've grown as a Christian and if you have any more discussions, please let me know."

"Rachel," replied Mr Watson, "it's been good to have you, and I'm sure we have all learned much by sharing together."

References

1,Matthew 13:2
2,Matthew 24:3
3,Matthew 23:2
4,Luke 18:13
5,Romans 5:3-4; Romans 8:17-18
6,2 Corinthians 4:17-18
7,Matthew 21:5; Matthew 11:29
8,Galatians 5:22-23
9,Matthew 9:36
10,1 John 3:17
11,1 John 4:20
12,James 2:14-17
13,Mark 12:30
14,Matthew 9:4
15,Hebrews 4:12
16,1 John 1:8
17,1 Corinthians 13:12
18,James 3:17
19,James 4:1-2
20,Hebrews 13:20
21,Isaiah 9:6
22,Colossians 1:20
23,1 Peter 4: 12-14

Also from Day One

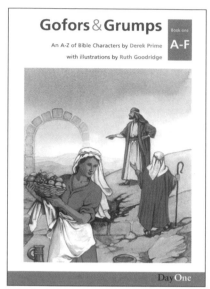

ABC 1

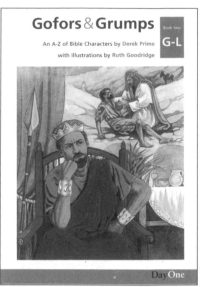

ABC 2

ABC 3

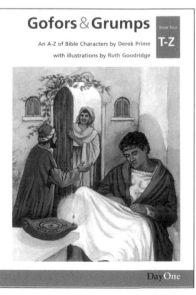

ABC 4

Gofors & Grumps

Derek Prime

When a thing is worthwhile doing, we sometimes say, "Go for it!" In the Bible many people wanted to please God, while plenty of others wanted their own way instead of God's. Derek Prime calls them Gofors and Grumps in a new series of four books designed for Children aged 7 to 11 years. The books use all the letters in the alphabet to describe characters in the Bible, from Mr Afraid (Adam) through to Mr Zoo-keeper (Noah), showing children how we can learn from their lives. Each book is full of useful learning exercises to occupy younger readers. There is a Bible dictionary in each book, together with maps and fact boxes, all well presented and superbly illustrated. An ideal gift for teaching the young.

£2.50 each

Special offer

Buy the first three in the series, and we will give you the fourth completely free! Normal price for the set of four is £10.00. Special price: £7.50 for the set of four while stocks last.

For further information, call or write to us—or find us on the web

☎ 01372 728 300

In Europe: ++ 44 1372 728 300
In North America: 011 44 1372 728 300
Day One   3 Epsom Business Park Kiln Lane Epsom Surrey KT17 1JF England
E–Mail: sales@dayone.co.uk

www.dayone.co.uk

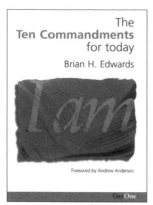

◀ "Edwards' book finds a well deserved place at the cutting edge of application of this important theme."

The Banner of Truth Magazine

The Ten Commandments for today

Brian H. Edwards

Large format paperback
288 pages

£8.99

At a time when the nation's morality is in alarming decline, it is surprising that so little has been written on the Ten Commandments. Brian Edwards gives us a modern commentary, carefully uncovering their true meaning and incisively applying them to our contemporary society.

Reference: IOT
ISBN 0 902548 69 7

The Lord's Prayer for today

Derek Prime

Large format paperback
163 pages

£5.95

The Lord's Prayer is the only pattern prayer the Lord Jesus provided and is timeless in purpose and function. It indicates how we are to pray throughout our life in this present world. It is essential for us to be reminded of its truths which do not change. The Lord's Prayer reminds us, at its very beginning, that true worship of God arises from a living relationship with Him as our Father through our Lord Jesus Christ.

Reference: LP
ISBN 0 902548 68 9